THROW LDREN

Abby's
Story

THROWN AWAY CHILDREN

Abby's Story

Louise Allen

with Theresa McEvoy

MIRROR BOOKS

First published by Mirror Books in 2020

Mirror Books is part of Reach plc
10 Lower Thames Street
London EC3R 6EN

www.mirrorbooks.co.uk

Print ISBN 978-1-913406-16-5
eBook ISBN 978-1-913406-15-8

Typeset by Danny Lyle

Printed and bound in Great Britain by
CPI Group (UK) Ltd, Croydon, CR0 4YY

A CIP catalogue record for this book is available from the British Library.

1 3 5 7 9 10 8 6 4 2

Cover image: iStock
(Posed by model)

To yours and my children.

If you understand and can feel the pain caused
by poverty and bad choices both here in real life or
in the institutions of the corporate parent, I beg you to
support our children and young people without ego
and self-interest. Instead, let's collectively do all
we can to genuinely help our children thrive.

Contents

Part One

Part One

I

Noise echoes around the gymnasium. The artificial light is bright and unforgiving.

Dozens of secondary school children dressed in identical pale blue polo-shirts and navy shorts dart about in organised chaos. Old-fashioned climbing apparatus stands dormant against the walls. The air is filled with shrieks, the squeaky noise of rubber trainers, and the thwack of nylon strings on shuttlecocks.

Lisa is in the middle of it all, down on the hard wooden floor, snatching desperately at a breath she can't seem to get hold of.

'What's up? Can't you take the pace? Is my killer drop shot too much for you?' Simone calls out to her from the other side of the net.

On any normal day Lisa would have a smart reply for Simone's banter, but today, right now, in this truly horrible moment, nothing whatsoever comes into her mind apart from trying to find that breath. The fact that she has no air in her lungs makes reply impossible anyway. She closes her eyes for a moment, focusing on the complicated act of breathing and on controlling the sharp, sharp pain that stabs suddenly through her side.

When she opens her eyes again Lisa has trouble focusing on the other three badminton courts. There are doubles games going on around her, in varying degrees of competitiveness, but she can't make them out properly. Something odd seems to have happened to her vision. Everyone and everything has a blurred edge, as though some distorting filter has been applied to reality.

She feels totally detached from everything. It is almost as though Lisa is no longer physically in the room, not part of this PE lesson. Perhaps the only way through this nightmare now is to pretend that it isn't happening, she thinks. To carry on pretending, as she has done for the last six months, ever since the horrible truth dawned on her. Only six months because it took her a long time to know. Barely pubescent, and having only just started in Year 8, she wasn't even having regular periods – so it took a while to notice that she wasn't having them at all.

Darting movements accompany the noise of laughter and whistles that continue to echo around the gym. Wednesday, period three. Double PE. Badminton. The world, school, is carrying on in the ordinary way that it does. Ordinary things are happening all around her.

But things are also happening *to* her. And those things are anything but ordinary.

Lisa finally manages to draw a breath from somewhere. She feels as though she is being pulled underwater but has snatched air at the surface. Nothing looks real. The whole room – the gym – also seems to be underwater. She can make out limbs and their bodies moving around the court spaces, but they look like insects, or seaweed – indistinct and inhuman. As do the students lined up on benches at the side, awaiting their turn to play. They are little dark blobs on the edge of her vision, not people at all.

Ms Plant – with the emphasis firmly on 'Ms' – is there in the corner; Lisa can just about identify the teacher through squinting eyes bracing against pain. But butch Ms Plant isn't even sympathetic to a bit of period pain, so she isn't going to be an ally. She can't see the whistle strung below Ms Plant's neck but knows it is there, as it is every PE lesson. She knows that she will get into serious trouble in a minute, if she doesn't get up. Ms Plant hasn't seen her yet. The teacher is busy looking at something in her hand. Maybe a stopwatch. Yes. Stopwatch.

Time.

It is nearly lunchtime. *Hold on to that thought,* she tells herself. Lunchtime. Perhaps the brutal, stabbing pain that Lisa feels in her stomach is just hunger. It could be. Some food might sort all this out. That will be it: food. But there is a similar sharp pain to the one in her abdomen over her right eye. That can't be from hunger. It feels as though someone has put an ice pick through her forehead and is twisting it around. She should take some paracetamol or ibuprofen. It is part hangover, perhaps. And part just having to deal with Year 9 PE, in her state. Usually exercise makes the pain go away. Not today.

'Get up, faker.'

Lisa hears Simone's voice but can't quite see her opponent and friend across the net, and can't seem to lift herself from the ancient parquet flooring. *Jesus. What the bloody hell is happening to me?* she thinks. *Get a grip. Everyone's looking.*

'Sorry, Lis – I didn't realise you were actually hurt. Did you twist something?' The voice is nearer now. Simone's tone has changed entirely and her face is wearing a concerned frown as she finally reaches Lisa. But Simone's approach also means that other people will notice.

Lisa gives up the struggle to focus properly. There is no point: nothing will stay still. The students on and near the benches seem to be floating in the air, not sitting or walking at all. Now some of them are running forward to be near her.

'Miss, miss! I think Lisa's fainted.'

But she has not fainted. She is still acutely conscious, and that consciousness carries the weight of a terrible fear. The pain recedes, momentarily. She manages to heave herself into a sitting position. Where is she? How has she ended up here? That's right, it is a PE lesson. She has been playing badminton with Simone. She had Maths and Geography before break. She is in school. It is nearly lunch. She just needs to get up. That's all. Stand up. Put the weight on to her feet. Lisa has found herself coaching herself like this at the most difficult moments for a while now. For the last few months at least. She recites tiny, ordinary details like a litany. Reminding herself what day it is, where she is, who she is.

All the while blocking out the *other* reality that she is fighting.

Now Ms Plant is kneeling down beside her. The ruddy face, open pores and sagging chicken neck come into sharp focus too suddenly, inches in front of her eyes. The dangling whistle is right in her face. *How bloody embarrassing.* She hates causing a fuss; being the centre of attention is highly undesirable when you are 13.

'What's going on here, Lisa? What's happened? Are you hurt? Is everything alright?'

'Miss, I'm fi—' Lisa's control over speech disintegrates and the sentence turns into a scream. She can't help herself, as the next wave of pain threatens to eat her up.

Jesus Christ, this can't be 'it', can it? Please no. Please no. Not here, not now, not in front of everyone.

And now the whole class has gathered round, like Lisa is the star attraction in a street performance, about to perform a dramatic stunt. And Plant is still peering right into her. Too close. It reminds Lisa of getting her eyes tested and having the optician eyeball to eyeball breathing into her face. She needs air, she needs space. She needs to be anywhere but here.

'Simone, run along to the medical room, will you? Get someone down here straight away.'

Simone is already on the move but Ms Plant is panicking, and uncharacteristically indecisive.

'No, come back, Simone; on second thoughts, you go instead, Melody. Simone, you stay here so that you can tell me exactly what happened. Did she get hit by a racquet? Did she slip? How did she end up on the floor?'

Simone looks utterly bewildered, shakes her head, shrugs. She has no real answers. Why should she? Lisa hasn't confided in her.

'I just don't know, Miss. I was just about to serve. She was all fine one minute and then she just sort of... collapsed.'

Lisa knows it isn't fair on her friend to be questioned like this. She hasn't told Simone anything. Poor Simone has no idea at all. And Lisa wants to reply for herself, to answer Ms Plant's questions, she really does; but the breathing thing – it's all she can concentrate on. It is as though her body is attacking her from the inside.

And, oh God, suddenly there is water, and blood, pooling out of Lisa, and spreading into a vast ocean across that parquet floor. She doubles up again in pain and vomits into the streaks of liquid forming around her. The vomit smells faintly of alcohol, but vodka, as she has learned, leaves only the faintest of traces and is easily masked.

It must be clear, even to Ms Plant, with her limited gynaecological knowledge, what is happening now.

The baby comes quickly. The paramedics only just make it.

There is time only to evacuate the rest of the class into a nearby classroom when Ms Plant, having sussed what is going on so unexpectedly with one of her pupils, tries to regain some kind of control of the situation. Three decades in teaching have not prepared her for this kind of emergency. 29 other students in Lisa's class hear the howls – of pain, of shame, of horror – from along the hallway.

There are giggles and gossip in the corridors and changing rooms and surrounding classrooms. Phrases bandied about that are only half understood by the students that say them.

'Was that her waters breaking?'

'So disgusting.'

'She had a baby during PE!'

'Did you see the mess it made?'

'Who do you think the father is?'

'Dirty bitch!'

'I didn't even know she was pregnant, did you?'

'Do you think it's someone in Year 9?'

'She had started to look a bit fat…'

'Did *you* know about this, Simone? You're her mate. She must have told you, surely?'

'Lisa doesn't even have a boyfriend, does she?'

'Perhaps it is another immaculate conception – the second coming!'

Lisa hears nothing of this, but she can guess.

And so a child is born in the middle of that gymnasium on a Wednesday afternoon during a double Year 9 PE lesson to a desperate teenage mother – an event heard by the rest of her class, and broadcast to the rest of the school in increasingly embellished tales, as if the reality isn't dramatic enough.

The baby is a girl. A tiny, little girl who weighs less than three pounds, and does not cry when she is born.

Lisa refuses to hold her, or even look at the *thing* that has come out of her. She shakes her head and turns away, stroking the parquet flooring instead. Now they want to take her to the hospital. They are worried about the baby. And her, of course. She is not interested in the baby, and certainly not interested in being its mother. She refuses to speak, refuses to actually acknowledge what has happened. Refuses on some level, even now, to believe it.

She is in a state of shock. Both at the horror of giving birth in such a traumatic way, and the trauma of having supressed the reality of her pregnancy ever since she discovered it.

The ambulance takes Lisa and the baby away to hospital.

A river of faces gawp through the classroom windows as the ambulance leaves the school site. They do nothing, just as they did nothing when Lisa lay labouring in the gym. Being watched in shock and horror and monstrous disbelief is something that will keep happening to her unfortunate child. For Lisa's classmates there is also delight in the drama of an interrupted lesson, a break from the routine.

For Lisa, so much more is broken – inside and out.

II

At the hospital there is still no peace. Why can't they just leave her alone? There are bright lights, difficult questions and probing fingers. Once the male doctor has been and checked her over, a nurse comes and brings her a cup of sweet tea. Lisa makes a face and spits the sickly liquid back into the cup immediately: she hasn't drunk tea with sugar since she was little.

'Drink it,' insists the nurse, as though it is some kind of potion that will take away the horror. It won't. Nothing can.

The feeling of detachment doesn't lift. Things continue to go on around Lisa, though she wants it all to just stop. There are phone calls, tears, utter disbelief.

Lisa's parents arrive.

They are concerned, of course, but also horrified and angry – and repulsed. Their daughter! She is only 13. Still a child herself.

'I told you we shouldn't have sent her to that school!'

It is typical of Lisa's mother to rake up an old argument to avoid dealing with the present one.

'I don't think it was the school who got her pregnant, do you?' Lisa's father says, acidly.

'But why didn't you tell us?'

Because of comments like that, thinks Lisa. Because, because. She still isn't ready to face the real reason that she couldn't tell them.

'And how can we have been so utterly clueless?' Lisa's mother goes on. 'I'd have noticed if you didn't wear such hideous, baggy, shapeless sweatshirts all the time. I thought it was a fashion statement, not a way to hide a *baby*!'

'It just seems incredible that you could keep this from us!'

Not just you, Lisa thinks. As well as her parents, she has somehow managed to keep the pregnancy secret from Simone, from her friends, from her teachers – from everyone else around her.

Her mother paces around the white floor tiles and talks about Lisa in the third person as though she isn't in the room. Lisa stops listening.

'But Clive, where did we go wrong with her? We gave her the best of everything. She is hard-working, high-achiev-ing. A model child. The perfect student at school. Glowing school reports, always! She comes from a good home, from a stable family... she's only 13! She should have her whole life ahead of her. And now...' her mother tails off, because the premature baby lying downstairs in the intensive care unit suggests otherwise. It suggests carelessness and promiscuity and a very different sort of picture from the one that Lisa's mother has of her daughter.

Lisa hangs her head in shame. She hasn't thought about anything much beyond the birth, about any kind of future. Her identity *is* bound up in being a good student. Her target grades for GCSEs are high and she has an exemplary school record to go alongside an excellent academic history. She knows this better than anyone. She doesn't need her mother to remind her of everything that has been lost. But her mother does remind her. Over and over again. She goes on and on.

She is a school prefect and plays the clarinet in the school orchestra. 'School prefects don't get pregnant! Musicians don't get pregnant! She is not the kind of girl to get pregnant. It is almost funny how they are focusing on the getting pregnant. Because she isn't pregnant anymore.

The questioning goes on, but they still talk about her as though she isn't in the room. '*How* has she given birth to a baby while still a few months short of her 14th birthday? I don't believe this has happened. *How* can this have happened? How can she have done such a thing?'

'I didn't *do* anything,' says Lisa, all of a sudden, tuning back in as she hears the blame start.

She can't be blamed for this.

'*I* didn't do anything.' She repeats the statement, more quietly and shifting the emphasis. They are about the first

14

words she has spoken voluntarily since that thing came out of her. And she realises how lame it sounds. But it is true – although she is still not ready to unburden herself from the secret she has harboured alone. It is a secret so painful that she hasn't even come close to explaining, even in her diary.

They are going to have to know, though. It is going to have to come out.

'I just couldn't tell you. I couldn't say the words out loud.'

Because really, how could she voice a truth that her mother would not be able to bear?

'What do you mean, *you* didn't *do* anything? Babies don't make themselves. It takes two to tango!'

'Let Lisa talk, love,' her father interjects.

She has *had* to keep this hidden, she tells them, finally through heaving sobs. 'I had no choice!' Lisa pauses and shudders. 'He made me…'

But the admission is so much that she breaks down again and can't say anymore.

Her mother gets her phone out to call the police. 'Oh darling, it was *rape*? Why didn't you tell us! Rape is a crime. It must be reported…'

'Wait, love,' says Lisa's father. 'Let's see what more Lisa has to say.' He senses now that the defilement of his daughter isn't the worst part of this nightmare saga.

But she has nothing more to say for the moment. Somehow Lisa falls asleep. It is both extreme fatigue and a defence mechanism. She is worn down by their questions and anger and tears and love, as well as the exhaustion of giving birth.

When she wakes up again a couple of hours later, Lisa knows that it is finally time to speak the truth. She has run out of options. She doesn't want to tell them the next part, but her parents will have to be the ones to hear it. She has no one else to tell, because Simone isn't able to visit her in the evening. In fact, she isn't able to visit her at all. Simone's parents have forbidden her from seeing Lisa, having heard a version of events that don't paint Lisa in a particularly good light. They don't want their own daughter tarnished by the scandal.

Lisa's parents themselves are already full of guilt at not having noticed what was going on. They are more sympathetic now. They reassure her that it doesn't matter how it happened. They will support her. Lisa is not so sure. They haven't heard the worst yet.

Her terrible, shameful secret: the child is Uncle Jason's.

Through sobs, Lisa reveals every last hideous detail of the secret that has been so difficult to bear, that has ripped her apart emotionally, and then torn her apart physically, and will now tear her family apart entirely.

The father is Lisa's uncle, her own mother's brother, Jason. Uncle Jason. She manages to bring the hated name to her lips a second time. Uncle Jason, who meted out his 'special cuddles' to his niece. She hadn't really known what was happening to her when she was raped by Jason, the weekend of her 13th birthday celebrations, when all the family stayed in caravans down at Camber Sands. She is calmer now that she is finally telling the story. She can separate herself from being at the centre of this narrative as she tells it.

'He picked a moment when there was no one around to hear the shouts. I couldn't tell anyone because he's your *brother*!'

Lisa had no idea that she was pregnant until it was way too late to do anything about it. She didn't really understand the changes that were happening to her barely ready body as she went through the middle stages of the pregnancy. She didn't even really suspect that she was in labour until moments before the baby arrived. She has been dealing with it all by pretending it is not there.

But there is one last thing that she is still not able to say out loud. She has spent the last few months drinking heavily, in secret. She has drunk herself into oblivion over and over again. First in an attempt to abort the baby, and then in an effort to block out the misery.

She doesn't want this baby.

She can't look after this baby.

She wants nothing to do with this baby.

She will never be able to love this baby.

'We'll put the baby up for adoption immediately,' her mother decides. 'We can make this right. It will be as though it never happened.'

Although of course, it won't.

There are signatures, and more forms to be filled out. It is a practical thing that can be done amidst all the tears and disgust and shouting and blame. It is a way out of this shocking mess.

The nurse comes back in to take away the cup of sweet tea that has gone cold. She replaces it with a fresh one, checks Lisa's pulse, holding her soft dark skin against Lisa's pale, bony wrist while she does it.

Her mother barely registers the nurse's arrival. They must have a name on the forms. Would Lisa like to name the baby, if not hold her?

Lisa looks ahead of her. She really can't bring herself to care. She toys briefly with the idea of naming the baby 'Simone' but decides that would not be fair on her friend. The nurse's badge is right in her face as she collects the tea. It says 'Abimbola'. It looks like a nice collection of sounds together. It must come from far away (in fact, the nurse is Nigerian on a short-term NHS contract). It has an exotic resonance that feels miles from this London suburb and Lisa wants to be just anywhere else but here in her own reality.

Abimbola. Lisa has never seen that collection of vowels and consonants in that order together as a name before, but there is a pleasing rhythm to it. And a nice circularity beginning and ending in that 'a' sound. It soothes Lisa to think about these things in an abstract way as words and letters, rather than to think about a baby as a living thing – or what her body has just been through.

Abimbola seems kind. She pushes the second cup of tea towards Lisa a fraction. Determined, without being pushy.

Lisa takes a sip. It tastes better this time. She allows the sweet liquid to trickle down her throat.

'A name,' her mother insists. 'We need a name for the form.'

Abimbola takes Lisa's temperature and makes a little clicking sound with her tongue when she registers a figure that is slightly higher than she would like. But she doesn't frown at her, or make a judgement or look pityingly at her – as everyone else has.

A-bim-bo-la. Lisa distracts herself while they take her blood pressure for the umpteenth time. She says it aloud and at different speeds and breaks the word down into its component parts.

It sounds beautiful. And different.

Lisa feels only indifference, but perhaps if any good at all can come from this unholy mess that has been created, then it needs a fresh start. 'It' being the baby. It needs an opportunity not to make the mistakes that Lisa herself has already made.

'Her name is Abimbola,' she declares. 'There. Abimbola. You asked for a name, and that's it.' She says it carelessly – as though she might have shown more interest in choosing pizza toppings. She ignores the raised eyebrows. She has suffered much worse recriminations today.

She falls asleep once more. Really, what more can they ask of her now?

But there is so much that Lisa doesn't understand. She doesn't consider the consequences of giving a little white girl about to be put up for adoption such a distinctive, African name. She still doesn't realise that she has permanently damaged her own liver in an attempt to drink away the shame and sorrow – and baby. She won't find that out until a little later. She doesn't understand that through the drinking and her decisions she has already damaged two lives – hers and Abimbola's.

Very quickly the adoption agency have a match. There are formalities to go through, but they are confident that they can cut through many of the bureaucratic processes. They have found a caring couple desperate for their own child but unable to have one.

Abimbola is officially taken away the very next day. She will need to remain in hospital for a while until she has put on some more weight and her respiratory system is more stable. She will remain in intensive care and then she can be cared for in the baby unit at the hospital until the necessary documents are in place.

Lisa doesn't say goodbye to her. She has refused to bond with this child – inside or outside of her. She doesn't hold the baby once. She doesn't look at her. She never sees the almost translucent, glassy skin of the newborn. A baby so fragile she looks as if she might just break. She turns her face away when she hears that Abimbola has gone. She can be someone else's problem now.

A few miles away a young woman is delighted to get the call. It is a dream come true, the moment they have been waiting for. Yes, they can move fast to make the necessary preparations. The handover can take place as soon as the baby is healthy enough to leave the hospital. They can be ready to welcome her into their home almost immediately.

And that is where Abimbola's problems truly begin.

III

Sarah busies herself around the sitting room, waiting for Gordon to come home from work. He won't be long now. She plumps up cushions that don't need plumping. She shuffles a stack of papers and magazines that are already neatly organised on the coffee table, moving *The Catholic Herald* to underneath the parish newsletter for better size order in the pile. She dusts imaginary flecks from ornaments on an immaculate mantlepiece, pausing to check her appearance in the large oval mirror that hangs above the fireplace. There is more colour in her cheeks than she has seen in a long time.

Toad-in-the-hole is cooking in the oven, the batter rising nicely the last time she peered through the glass door. A pan of Sarah's special onion sauce simmers gently on the hob through its final reductions: it is Gordon's favourite mid-week meal. She checks her watch again, an automatic, if unnecessary action; she has timed it all to perfection as usual and Gordon is never late.

A bottle of good red wine is breathing on the dining table. Sarah made a special trip to the new Waitrose and spent more money than she intended on a Châteauneuf-du-Pape. They are an abstemious household as a rule, but tonight is a special occasion and they will both enjoy a glass with the meal. Gordon will not object once he understands what it is that they are celebrating. She smooths over one of the two folded linen napkins, already immaculately ironed into perfect triangles, brushes away a non-existent speck and places a box of matches near the candlesticks, so that they are all ready to be lit at precisely the right moment.

The seconds tick by with an agonising slowness.

Finally, there it is: the sound of Gordon's key turning in the lock. She rushes to the hall when she hears the familiar metallic click so that she is there to reach for the coat that is folded over his arm.

'Welcome home, dear. Good day?'

She hangs the coat in the hall cupboard, before turning to kiss his proffered cheek.

'Fair to middling.'

He always says this; a standard response no matter what might have happened during his working day as a commercial loss-adjuster in a large insurance firm in the next town. He is as predictable as the tides, as reliable as the Volvo that he drives there and back each day. You?'

'Very! In fact…' she is about to blurt it out – the news that is consuming her – but then pauses. It is too soon to tell him. 'I… have had a very good day.'

She must find the right moment to explain properly. She wants it to be perfect. It is such a big deal after all. They have been trying for a baby of their own for more than five years, almost all the time that they have been married. Half a decade of sadness and loss, punctuated from time to time with fleeting hope, quickly quashed.

Only recently has she been able to convince him that adoption really is the way forward, finally persuading him to embark on the lengthy administrative process that will get them there. Gordon was much keener on prayer than practical solutions, so she used his strong faith to help suggest that the losses they have suffered are God's way of telling them to choose a different path to parenthood in order to create the family they both long for so much.

'I will tell you all about it over dinner. Which I *think* you will enjoy,' she says, a little coyly.

'Well, something certainly smells good in here.' He moves over to the hob. 'And this looks like a significant clue as to what it might be.' He stirs the sauce with the wooden spoon that sits on the silicone rest beside the oven, before taking a teaspoon from the drawer to try a little on his tongue. 'Not bad!'

'Not bad' is a phrase that Sarah considers to be high praise indeed, coming from Gordon. It is a good start to their evening. She even finds that she isn't as irritated as usual by the back-seat cooking that he has such a tendency towards. But it is still too early to switch up to the next level of her campaign. She waits until he is seated at the table, grace has been said with appropriate solemnity, and dinner is served.

'So. I expect you are wondering what all of this is in aid of.'

She gestures to the wine and the good silver cutlery, polished this afternoon. Gordon looks up at her quickly and she sees the awful hope – and the corresponding fear – in his eyes. She realises what he must be thinking and knows that she must shut down *that* avenue quickly. Multiple pregnancies and miscarriages have taken their toll on him almost as much as they have on her. That unbearable hope is what makes it so devastating. They have had suppers like this before, though she had left it longer and longer to tell him about the thin blue line on the pregnancy test each time.

'No, no, darling. Don't worry. It's not *that* sort of news. I'm not expecting. Well, not exactly. But it is about our family. Our new family. I heard from the adoption agency today.' Sarah has planned to tell him slowly, but the excitement just bubbles up within her, uncontainable. 'We *are* going to be parents, Gordy. To a little baby girl!'

She only calls him Gordy in their most tender, private moments.

Gordon says nothing for a moment. Sarah looks into his face, searches his eyes to find the shining joy that she knows are in her own. But his expression is suddenly unreadable. Why? This is what they have wanted, what they have longed for. Isn't it? Finally his stern features break into a smile.

'That's great news, indeed, Sarah. We are blessed! Praise be to God.'

It is that little moment of hesitation before Gordon's response, and his characteristically religious declamation that inspire Sarah not to reveal the precise details of Abimbola's conception right now. That can wait. She can bide her time until the baby is settled into their household before revealing *that* part of Abimbola's story. He doesn't ask the question about why this baby is being put up for adoption directly, which means that Sarah can simply be flexible with the bare facts. Gordon's deep-rooted Christian beliefs and Old Testament philosophy will, she knows, make it difficult for him to come to terms with the baby's incestuous origins – but it will be his Christianity, also, that will allow him to welcome such a vulnerable and innocent child into their home.

For now, there are plenty of other things to think about. The practical details. Like the nursery, for starters. She rises from the table and fetches the designer paint cards that she collected on her way home from the supermarket. She has already spent an hour mesmerised by the squares of colour in their variegated shades.

'I'm thinking this "Caribbean morning dew" along with the "coral white". What do you think? I picked up some tester pots, too.'

She explains about Abimbola's name. 'It's very unusual, isn't it? Distinctive. I looked it up. It's a Yoruba tribal name. From somewhere in Africa. But she is white British in terms of her actual ethnicity. There may be a family connection to that part of the world, I suppose.' Sarah stops herself from launching into further speculations. Gordon doesn't like it when she talks too much – or 'witters on', as he sometimes terms it.

'And Abby is a lovely diminutive, isn't it? People will probably just think her name is Abigail!'

After Gordon has led the thanksgiving prayers, the rest of the evening is spent making what, for Sarah, are blissful plans: lists of purchases that will need to be made; whether it will be right to send out announcement cards to all their friends; possible choices for a fresh colour scheme in the utility room, as well as in the long dormant nursery. 'I'll be doing lots of laundry, now.' She talks away merrily in happy anticipation of what it will be like when Abby arrives with them, and she is desperate to share their news.

'Shall we phone your parents and tell them? They've been waiting a long time to become grandparents!'

The formalities are dealt with quickly by the relevant authorities: the adoption agency fall over themselves to push things through with this lovely, relatively wealthy couple. The domestic practicalities are managed in the same way by Gordon, who even takes some time off work to help with the shopping and decorating, and chooses a statue of the Virgin Mary with child as an ornament for Abimbola's room. Sarah swallows her thought about their baby's less-than-immaculate conception, and the adoption day comes round relatively fast in real terms. Abimbola has been in hospital for eight weeks but is now ready to come home for the first time, having reached a healthy, stable weight.

It hasn't felt fast for Sarah, who has experienced each day, each hour even, before being united with her new child as an agony. Mostly she has kept herself busy through a rigorous rota of spring-cleaning and organising. The house is like a show-home from the new estate. The floorboards are polished to a deep, rich shine. The curtains are dry-cleaned, room by room. A new changing station in the nursery is installed and filled with nappies and wipes and creams and oils and muslins and multiple romper-suits and vests and baby blankets. They are equipped, so she thinks, with everything that Abimbola could need, and more.

The health visitor eyes the overwhelming *order*, and somewhat unnatural lack of clutter, somewhat doubtfully when she makes a preliminary home visit.

'You know it's not going to *stay* like this, don't you? A baby brings chaos to a household! Your pristine furniture isn't going to stay like that for very long.'

Sarah nods. Of course she knows it isn't going to stay like this all the time. And she really does, in theory. She has a giant stack of books – every parenting manual and baby guide that has been published recently – on the nursery shelf, and she has read them all. She doesn't expect it to be easy. But she has yearned for this moment of holding her baby in her arms for so, so long. She just wants it all to be perfect.

When Abimbola – Abby – is finally passed to her, a deep maternal instinct kicks in so profoundly that Sarah feels as though she is the baby's one true mother. This tiny human life is now in her hands. Eight precious weeks old. And Abby was so small at birth that now, at two months, she is the size of a newborn. Sarah vows that she will make up for Abby's complicated start in life and all that time spent in hospital by providing for her every need. She is such a wonder to look at, truly an astonishing thing. Her wrinkled, puckered face with its squashy little nose is just adorable. Her eyes are very little and wide-set. Her miniature fingers and fingernails seem a magnificent feat of nature; the tiny toes look simply edible. They are all such a miraculous combination. A perfect package of baby. She wants to eat Abby up with love. She marvels at every detail of her.

'Oh Gordy, look!'

Abby makes little 'startle' reflex movements in her sleep. At the end of one of them, she clutches on to Sarah's little finger, balling her fist tightly round the digit.

'Will you look at that! She hasn't even opened her eyes to see you yet, but you are already bonding!' Gordon kisses his wife on top of her head and they look for all the world like proud new parents.

An ugly thought finds its way into Sarah's head as she cradles Abby in her arms. It is the nagging concern, well – more than a nagging concern, actually, if she is honest – surrounding the way that she has kept the details about

Abimbola's parentage from Gordon. It is deceptive. In her heart of hearts, she knows it is.

And she is terrified that one of the professionals will blurt it out accidentally before she has had a chance to tell him properly. She cuts off everyone by speaking over the top of them until Gordon frowns at her.

The weeks since they have known of Abby's arrival date should have given Sarah plenty of time to find the right moment; it's just that she never wanted to break the magical, joyful spell that had been cast as they got ready for the baby and prepared to enter the next chapter of their lives.

But each visit and check that they have to go through in the first month is painful for that reason. Sarah wills the social worker and the health visitor and the agency worker not to make any reference to it. It isn't that it is a *secret*, exactly, she tells herself. It just wouldn't be fair to dwell on it, for Abby's sake. There is no need to alert Gordy to it. Yet. She will find the moment.

And, even if Sarah was ready to tell, there isn't actually a moment anyway. Parenting is just so hard. Abby is unbelievably demanding, but it isn't surprising given the traumatic start she has had in life. Sarah just hasn't prepared herself for it to be as gruelling as she is finding it. First there are the sleepless nights. She expected those, of course. She has read in one of her books that some babies enter the world back to front with their nights as days and days as nights. It makes a kind of sense when you consider that she's spent the last nine months in the darkness of the womb, rather than working around a day and night timetable. And being on the baby ICU ward at the hospital, it can't have been easy to distinguish night from day. But none of the parenting tips from the mountain of manuals seem to be having any effect at nudging Abby in the right direction.

And worse than the nights are the days. Sarah really wasn't expecting the *days* to be quite so full-on as well. Abby is a 'difficult' baby, she is told when she discusses her behaviour with the social worker, because she was born 'in such difficult circumstances.' Patience is the only solution, she is told. Rather patronisingly, in Sarah's opinion.

Oddly, Abby doesn't seem to be able to go for more than a couple of hours without feeding – day or night. But she was so underweight when she arrived in the world that perhaps this is just a necessary part of her growth. It doesn't seem to make much difference to her weight, though. In spite of feeding all the time, she barely seems to put any more weight on. Sarah has noticed that she is very restless, even when she does sleep for short, precious hours. And the crying! She rages against the world all the time. It is as though nothing is ever right in Abby's world. Her rages leave Sarah as burned out as the baby is by them. She screams and screams for hours on end and Sarah can see her lips vibrate with the force of her cries. It is exhausting to deal with, exhausting to watch. Sarah reminds herself that it must be even more exhausting for Abby to go through. Her rages are frighteningly prolonged and seemingly inexplicable. Sarah tends to Abby's every possible need as best she can, but nothing seems to calm her.

After a while, Sarah puts Abby's evident distress down to her own inexperience as a mother. She begins to berate herself. She must have been wrong about the maternal instinct that she thought she felt when she first held her. She isn't cut out for this.

Sarah is just so lonely and she doesn't know what to do to stop Abby from crying. Because she wasn't in an antenatal group, she hasn't made the group of friends that she might have done. And she can't meet anyone because Abby is too difficult to take to any kind of group. They had to leave the 'baby yoga' class that she signed up for because the leader pointed out that they were upsetting the other babies.

The health visitor is worried by Abby's inability to put on any weight. She is off the bottom of the chart, now, in the little red book Sarah carries to the doctor's surgery each week to monitor growth. Abby is so underweight that she doesn't even register on their measurement scales. It is another thing to worry about. Another thing that brings guilt. She can't be feeding the baby right.

It is all made much more difficult by the fact that right from day one Gordon is unable to soothe Abby at all, no matter what he does. He has no idea – and no patience to try. And because he has to work he can't be up through the night. Sarah takes on virtually all of Abby's care from the outset. She might as well be a single parent. Everything is left to her. Every single night feed, and every torturous moment of every day, the onus is on her. Gordon tries, when he walks through the door some nights, to be of some help, but Abby's little body goes rigid against him, like she is pushing him away – and she screams even louder until she is returned to Sarah. There is no let up, no respite. Sarah knows that she is looking haggard. She has stopped looking at her reflection in the oval mirror above the fireplace. If she does accidentally catch sight of herself she gives herself a fright.

Gordon seems to become more and more awkward each time he tries to hold his adopted daughter; he can't understand why he can't get it right. And he has the strangest feelings towards her, he tells Sarah. 'It is almost as though I am becoming – indifferent – is the best way that I can describe it. I have prayed and prayed to God for help.' He doesn't tell Sarah that he feels as though a shell is growing around his heart. He is unable to feel anything at all for this child, this miracle that for so long they longed for. It would destroy Sarah to know that.

Only a few weeks into the motherhood journey, Sarah feels utterly exhausted. It no longer feels like a journey, because there is no sign of any destination. She is shattered by the whole thing. She has never known tiredness like it. Ever. There seems no end to it. It is one big battle to abate the constant crying. She falls asleep sometimes when she is feeding Abby; she never means to, but she feels her eyelids closing and her head nodding and is powerless to do anything about it. The odd snatched moments of dozing, even if they are sitting up on the sofa, then seem to leave her even more tired than before – and guilt-ridden, in case any harm should come to Abby.

All the domestic preparations she made with the house have left Sarah herself ill-prepared physically and emotionally for this enormous undertaking. She had thought herself so ready, before the baby came. *Has it all been a terrible mistake?* she wonders, and then berates herself once more for acknowledging that thought. But something feels very, very wrong inside her. Can you get post-natal depression if you haven't actually given birth to the child? Is that possible? Why does she feel like this? Like she could burst into tears at any moment? Like there is no hope in anything? She wants to cry every time that Abby does. Her head hurts all the time and her breasts feel tender – almost as if she could feed the baby herself. But of course, that is ridiculous. Her symptoms must be psychosomatic. She's heard of a condition where the partner experiences the same pregnancy symptoms as a woman – perhaps it is something like that. She will look it up when she has a moment, which feels like it will be never.

Sarah knows that she also puts unnecessary demands on herself in trying to keep the house in perfect condition. The way Gordon likes it to be. She is anxious to minimise the disruptions to his work and to his prayer; after all, it is she who has pushed for this baby.

Meanwhile Gordon can see that the baby is eating Sarah up emotionally and tearing her apart physically and he has no idea what to do, other than pray for her – and for Abby, for them all. He consoles himself by re-reading verses from Matthew over and over: whoever welcomes a child in Christ's name welcomes Christ. But the shell around his heart continues to harden in spite of his increasingly frequent entreaties to the Lord. Perhaps it would have been easier with a son.

Abby is five months old and has been with them for three months when Sarah is in the supermarket buying nappies one day. They go through such a lot, because she changes Abby even when she doesn't need it – just in case she does. It is something to *do* when Abby is engaged in one of her endless rages. Sarah walks past the feminine hygiene products in one aisle and feels annoyed that they are so close to where the nappies are on the shelves. Only a man would do that, she thinks, deciding that the store layout must have been designed by a man. But the connection between the two things leaves her noticing that it has been a while since she has actually bought any tampons herself. She wonders if your periods can stop *as though* you have given birth when you become an adoptive mother. She can't quite work out how long it has been, now that she stops to think about it, but she certainly hasn't had one since Abby arrived. Then she has another thought.

A mad thought, but it would help explain the colossal tiredness. The tenderness and the soreness. The nausea that she has been calling tiredness for weeks. It couldn't be, could it?

35

She has multiple pregnancy tests stashed at the back of the bathroom cupboard, but she buys another one anyway. She used to do them regularly before they were 'blessed' with Abby, even when she knew that there was no possible way that she could be pregnant.

Gordon is already home when she walks through the door clutching a bag of shopping in one hand and balancing the handle of the car seat with Abby strapped inside with the other arm.

'Hi Gordon. How was your day?' she asks, raising her voice over the top of Abby's screeching – the sound that has become the soundtrack to their lives.

'Fair to middling, fair to middling.'

Lucky you, she thinks, unable to remember the last time she could describe one of her days as 'fair to middling'.

'Right. Just take her for a moment, will you?'

She doesn't even take off her coat before locking herself into the downstairs bathroom with the shopping bag. She rips the device from its packaging in a kind of frenzy, but she already knows. This time the blue line that she had always anticipated so eagerly and had so often eluded her, forms within seconds – she doesn't need to wait out the time. Oh God.

'Gordon,' she calls, weakly.

IV

Charles is a much, much easier baby – right from the moment he is born. Sarah is ridden with guilt and blames herself for the very obvious contrast between her two children, and for what she hopes is a less obvious contrast in her feelings for them. She carried this one; over 40 weeks she shaped and bonded with Charlie, her darling boy. Previous unsuccessful pregnancies have taught her the terror of carrying a child, but this time it felt different as soon as she found out she was pregnant. And perhaps it was made all the easier because of not knowing that she was pregnant for nearly eight weeks – firstly because she didn't think that she *could* be pregnant, and secondly because she had been too caught up with caring for Abby and exhausted by her constant demands to notice anything very much about herself. All of which meant that the first scan came within a few weeks of finding out the news. There was none of the anxious turmoil that dominated her earlier pregnancies. She realises now that she must have already been in the early stages of pregnancy very soon after

Abby first came to live with them. If only she had known. If only they had waited. The simple fact is that Sarah loves this child, Charles, more than Abby, who is simply so difficult just to be with. It is a hard, hard thing to admit to, even privately. Impossible to articulate aloud. And very un-Christian, she keeps reminding herself.

At 10 months old now, Charlie is peaceful, all the time. He has such a relaxed, easy-going manner. So serene in comparison to his adopted sister: he sleeps, he smiles, he oozes happiness and fulfilment. Abby remains almost always rage-filled. Her top lip curls up in a sneer so that she always looks as if she is on the verge of crying. She can never get enough of *anything* to satisfy her, let alone please her. She is an angry bundle of baby, even today, when they are celebrating her second birthday.

Sarah feels fully attuned to Charles' needs, and finds herself echoing the little noises of contentment that the baby makes when they are snuggled up together. That never happened with Abby, simply because there has never seemed to *be* any contentment. Sarah has thought about this a lot in the intervening months since Charles arrived in the family and she has had the chance to experience motherhood in an entirely different way. It is almost as if there is something profoundly wrong with Abby. And indeed, she hasn't really reached any of the milestones that are supposed to happen. At 24 months she can coast around the sitting room holding onto furniture, but can't walk independently yet, which makes trying to go anywhere with two 'babies' virtually impossible. Most babies take their first steps at around a year. She is still very small for her age, and hasn't really started making the sounds that she should do by now – other than screaming. She is very, very good at that. Charles seems at least as mobile and perhaps more advanced in terms of his communication skills, even though he is more than a year younger.

It must be, Sarah has concluded, that all the aggression and rage that Abby demonstrates is not all that surprising, to be expected given her terrible origins, that conception in the most obscene, sinful way. Sarah realises that she sounds like Gordon when she uses those kind of words. But Abby has every right to be angry at the world. She has every right to be a kind of 'devil-child'. That's how Sarah reminds herself not to blame Abby for her behaviour, especially when Gordon does. It is why she tries even harder to make things right for her, to make up for the love that she doesn't feel, but should. Abby has never stopped being 'difficult', even if it is with good reason. The difficulties she generates have just changed over time to incorporate new, impossible demands.

Perhaps, in fact, the rush of maternal love that she thought she felt for Abby initially was no more than the first pregnancy hormones of her own baby boy fizzing around inside her. Because Sarah has never known an all-consuming love like that she feels for Charlie. She can't help but wish sometimes that they just didn't *have* Abby. She feels more than ever that Abby is an outsider, not one of them, not a 'real' part of the family. But that, in itself, is such an uncharitable thought. What chance would a child like Abby have in the world if it wasn't for Gordy and Sarah taking her in? Gordy *still* doesn't know the full truth about his adopted daughter being the result of incestuous rape. He wouldn't find it at all easy to deal with and Sarah has felt, as time went on, that it was kinder simply not to tell him. Especially when nobody else mentioned it. His Christian sensibilities would struggle so much to process that knowledge, especially when Abby was so challenging, and so hard to love anyway. And after a certain amount of time had passed, there never *could* be a good moment to share that news. It would have seemed deceitful, as though she had deliberately concealed the knowledge from Gordon in an underhand way. Which, she supposed, she had – but only with the best intentions.

This morning, on her second birthday, Abby has a session at the nursery for a couple of hours. She has been going a couple of times a week since Charles was born, to give Sarah a little break and time to spend with her son. The gorgeous one-to-one time that Abby's absence gives her with Charlie has become something of a craving for Sarah. It is so full of pleasurable sensation. Today, though, she must spend the time getting ready for Abby's birthday tea-party this afternoon. There is plenty to do. Sarah can spend hours just gazing at her son's flawless features while he is sleeping, and loves watching all the little developments that happen when she plays with him, so she really must force herself to do all the jobs that need doing before the celebration, before three o'clock when the other guests will arrive.

She does allow herself a few moments of gazing at her son, though. Next to Charles, all Abby's defects are writ large. The too-small and too-far-apart eyes, the smooth skin above her top lip, her head slightly too large for her body, like she hasn't quite grown into it − all the unique things about Abby that were so endearing and distinctive in the beginning are characteristics that they now suspect to be the product of foetal alcohol syndrome, something that the doctor keeps shortening to 'FAS', which sounds far less damaging. There are some tests you can do. Abby might need some kind of therapy.

Sarah has done a bit of digging into Abby's past, as much out of desperation as concern. The poor teenage mother had been drinking through the pregnancy, to try and 'destroy' the child, it has since emerged. Sarah wonders how they didn't know that when Abby was born. Perhaps they did. The signs must have been there. Would she and Gordon have taken her in if they had known that at the time? It's a difficult question. Sarah knows how desperate she was for a baby. *If only she had known that one would soon be on the way.*

Charles. Her 'real' one.

Gordon is so much easier around Charles, too. He can hold his son without looking awkward and like it is an effort. He delights in his baby chatter and laughs at the facial mimicry, the little things that Abby never really did as a baby. Charles never goes rigid against his father, or throws a tantrum if Gordon goes near him.

Gordon knows the part about the drinking habits of Abby's mother, now, and it hasn't helped his disposition towards his adopted daughter in the slightest. If anything, it has made things worse. It really only all began to come to light fully after the first few appointments with the health visitor, when it was clear that Abby wasn't growing at quite the rate she should and they began to look more closely at the little developmental delays that Sarah had noticed. Though it helps to explain many of Abby's behaviours, Gordon hasn't taken the news very well. Lately he has become obsessed by the youth of Abby's mother. He brought it up again at dinner last night – dinner that he had to sit at the table by himself to eat, because Sarah was busy feeding Charles, and Abby was busy causing her usual chaos. Sarah has taken to leaving her to eat separately in the kitchen and then just cleaning up the disaster area afterwards. Mealtimes are just easier that way. She has kitted out the kitchen with wipe-down vinyl sheets covering virtually everything. No longer does she expose the lovely bespoke shaker cabinets so carefully chosen just a few years ago. She looks back at that version of her that was so house-proud and barely recognises it. Meanwhile she also has to deal with Gordon's mania about Abby's birth mother.

'A sinning, fornicating child herself. No wonder her offspring is such a monster.'

Sarah had bridled at the term 'offspring'. It sounded so detached. And the poor girl had hardly been 'fornicating', but Gordon doesn't know that.

Part of his anger on some subliminal level, she knows, is actually more to do with Sarah herself and her all-consuming relationship with Charles, but he can't show it. Between the demands of caring for Abby and Charles there is no time for Gordon. Sarah never guessed while she was pregnant that she would feel so physically broken after the birth. She isn't nearly ready to be physically intimate with her husband yet, and she knows that this is making him cross, though he would never express his frustration at her directly. Instead, he takes it out on Abby as his resentment grows. And grows. And grows.

Which is why Abby shall have an extra-special birthday party today, thinks Sarah. We can try, for just one day, to play happy families. There is bunting, there is cake, there are balloons. There is even a game of pass-the-parcel, all sello-taped up and ready to go, though Sarah admits to herself that it might be too much to ask that a group of two-year-olds sit in a circle and follow the rules for long enough to play the game. Still, she has done her best. She has 'Baby Mozart'

CDs at the ready. She is trying all the time to find ways to help stimulate Abby's delayed development.

The doorbell rings.

It will be the contractors on the new extension. With two children now – *two* children, whoever would have thought – they are in need of an extra bedroom. They have decided to build out over the flat roof at the back of the house to create the extra space they are going to need as the children grow up. The architects did their job well. Planning permission was pushed through much more quickly than they had expected and work can begin next week. Charles will need his own room once Sarah has finished nursing him, and the thought of returning to Gordon's bed doesn't appeal at all. She is still breast-feeding, proud that she has managed to go on much longer than most of her friends.

She places Charles gently – and reluctantly – down on his little play mat. He makes no fuss, just gazes up at his mother and smiles at her as though he is drinking her face in. She is thinking about putting him up for a modelling agency. He is so gorgeous. Sarah loves that look he gives her, and wants to show the world. Abby would have screamed at being put down like that at his age. Still would, in fact. Sarah sighs and goes to open the door.

Victor introduces himself. He is to be the foreman on the extension job. They shake hands in a rather formal way – his hands are warm, and enfold hers completely – and she welcomes him into the house, offering to put the kettle on. He is a little younger than her, perhaps 30ish, with dark blonde hair. He looks lightly dishevelled in his worn combat trousers, in what Sarah admits to herself is a startlingly attractive way. Not so dishevelled as to be unkempt, but enough to look like he might need a little bit of looking after. Sarah is surprised to have even noticed these details, so wrapped up has she been in Charles since his birth.

They talk awkwardly while the kettle boils: Victor comments on the bunting, Sarah explains about the birthday party in the afternoon. But even with the awkwardness, Sarah is energised by their conversation. She would like to run her hands through that slightly rumpled hair, to smooth it down, she realises, or run her hand along that stubbled jawline. She is slightly shocked at her own reaction to him: she hasn't had anything approaching a sexual thought since Charles was born. She doesn't know that she has *ever* wanted to run her fingers through Gordon's hair, which is dark and slicked to the side and would never be even the slightest bit out of place.

Victor doesn't stay long; he is only checking over the plans and measurements and working out how they will get their equipment in around the back when work starts on Monday. It leaves Sarah alone with her confusing thoughts, a half-formed determination to 'get her mojo back', and the rest of the party preparations to occupy her.

It is soon time to collect Abby from the nursery. The time without her has passed Sarah by in a flash. She suppresses the counterpoint thought: time *with* Abby sometimes seems endless. But today is her birthday and she *will* have a nice day. Whatever happens, she will see to it. Sarah nods her way through the litany of misdemeanours that Abby has got up to in the short time since she dropped her off, letting them wash over her. She doesn't seem to be able to play nicely with any of the other children and just destroys their games. She isn't very good at sharing. She hurt another child. She won't sit down to eat and throws her food around. *Tell me something I don't know,* thinks Sarah. Today she has been throwing gravel at passers-by through the iron bars of the nursery playground railings. They've had a complaint. Well, that's a new one. Sarah knows, though, that she is the one who is being told off under the guise of 'chatting through Abby's day'. *But I didn't throw the bloody gravel,* she thinks. *And it isn't my fault. She isn't my creation. I didn't give birth to her!*

Sarah grits her teeth and manages not to get cross when Abby does the rigid-backed protest at being strapped into her car-seat when she tries to put her in the car. Sarah sings a lullaby over the top of her screeching all the way home, smiling at Charles in the rear-view mirror. He just seems to take it all in his stride. It is hard to stay upbeat, but she will. It's Abby's birthday. She is entitled to a day of fun.

The party is as much of a success as any social occasion with Abby can be. Sarah doesn't like to admit to herself that she is running out of mums who are happy to spend time with them. It is only Lindy and Karen, two friends from baby rhyme-time who have older children as well as their babies and don't really know Abby; and Sunita, another mum from nursery who brings her toddler, Jason, with her. The name makes Sarah uncomfortable for some reason, she doesn't know why. It just seems such an odd choice for a little boy.

Pass-the-parcel doesn't work terribly well, as Sarah suspected it wouldn't with a bunch of two-year-olds. It was always going to be ambitious. There is a tantrum when Abby, who doesn't seem capable of grasping even the basics of the game, doesn't get to take off a layer each time the music stops. Baby Mozart doesn't seem to be the calming influence that the online forums promised it would be. There are only so many times that Sarah can smile and shrug off Abby's behaviour. Sarah finds it liberating to repeat the thought that she isn't responsible. There is more rage when the parcel is down to its final layers and has become so small that Abby is not able to tear the paper at all without help. She is unimpressed with the cheap plastic toy inside; it is tossed aside almost immediately. All that effort, for nothing.

Next, she tries a game of 'Dead Lions'. Abby is out first, of course. She finds it impossible to be still, even for a second. Sarah is really rather regretting inviting anyone round at all. Perhaps they should have just marked Abby's birthday as a family and not got anyone else involved to witness the awfulness.

When it is time for the cake to come out, Gordon dims the lights and everyone sings 'Happy Birthday'. Sarah is proud of her handiwork: the sponge, carefully iced in blue, is in the shape of the Iggle Piggle character from *In The Night Garden*, one thing that sometimes keeps Abby calm for a few minutes in the evening. Abby is transfixed by the candles, but her brow creases into a frown and she suddenly plunges her fist into the icing and then hurls the cake away from her just at the moment that Gordon tries to take a picture. The hours of labour have simply served to create a blue squidgy mess on the floor.

Sarah laughs it off. 'Two-year-olds!' But inside she wants to cry. 'I didn't want any cake anyway – bad for the figure,' she jokes as she scrapes blue gunk from the rug.

Abby bursts into howling tears of outrage now that the cake is gone and it is clear that she isn't getting any. Her destruction was so complete that nothing of it can be salvaged. There is an embarrassed murmur of 'It's her party and she'll cry if she wants to!' from Sunita.

Gordon is busy wiping crumbs and clearing the smear on his camera lens. 'Shame I wasn't videoing that. We'd make a fortune on *You've Been Framed*!' He joins in the banter, but Sarah senses that he is furious about the state of his camera.

In the end, Sarah is just thankful when the whole ordeal is over and everyone departs.

She fancies a large glass of wine to celebrate once both babies are down for the evening, but she is still breast-feeding, so forces herself not to. Instead she sets about picking up the other food that has been dropped – and flung, in Abby's case – across the kitchen tiles.

She can't get the image of Abby punching her little fist through the cake and swiping it onto the floor out of her mind. The whole thing was an absolute disaster. A nightmare. And there isn't even a photograph of the bloody cake.

In the darkest spaces of her heart she knows that Charles could never, *would* never, behave as Abby does. At 10 months old, his temperament is just so different from Abby's. He was an angel at the party and had everyone cooing and fussing over him – when Abby should have been the star of the show. But she certainly made herself the centre of attention with the cake escapade.

And there is even more food mess to clear up than there should have been. Gordon, too, threw a plate across the room once everyone else had gone. He wasn't trying to *hit* Abby, Sarah is sure. Not to hurt her, she convinces herself. He was just lashing out, wildly – without specific direction. It was a natural reaction – just anger at the mess, and at his camera. Abby seems to have become the focus for much of his anger, lately, and that has begun to worry Sarah. Gordon's evident dislike of Abby is mutating into something darker. Is loathing too strong a word for Gordon's feelings towards his adopted daughter? Maybe not. Thank goodness he doesn't know all the details about Abby's conception. She has kept that secret for a long time now.

How is it possible that her world has become this? Sarah thinks, flinging lumps of uneaten birthday cake and half-chewed carrot sticks into the bin, surveying the wreckage of her kitchen.

She makes sure that Abby is booked in for a double session at nursery when she marks Charles' first birthday a couple of months later. It is an altogether much happier affair without 'the child from hell', as Gordon has lately dubbed her.

V

Sarah is very good at 'doing' Christmas, and this year she surpasses herself.

She has always had a knack for the little touches, the details that make everything just right, especially about the Christmas feast itself. She is good at ingredients. All the ingredients, not just the edible ones: a fabulous table decoration that coordinates with everything in the room, personalised hand-made place names, carefully chosen 'table gifts' to be unwrapped between courses, home-made crackers with individual treats selected for each guest, sculptured napkins artfully decorating plates and glassware, and silver cutlery polished to perfection. And of course she is also a marvellous cook, one who is never flustered because she is supremely organised and always prepares as much as possible in advance so that everything looks effortless on the big day.

As with the attention to detail on the table, she goes the full Heston Blumenthal in the food preparation. The carrots are glazed in orange and ginger, the sprouts are drizzled in pistachio and pomegranate, chestnuts have been roasted and will be dressed with crisp pancetta, and that is all before she comes to the pièce de résistance: the turkey. Last year she recreated the medieval royal five-bird roast, all boned and stuffed inside one another. She has kept it simpler this year. This year she is roasting her turkey with saffron. It will be a riotous assembly of Christmas flavours on the table. She has snatched hours when Charles is sleeping, or playing contentedly while Abby is at nursery, to make sure that everything is perfect. She styles herself as the consummate domestic goddess on these occasions (though Gordon would not actually approve of the term 'goddess') and this has become important for her sense of self. A self that she knows is being gradually eroded through the constant struggle to meet the needs of Charles between the demands of Abby, all the while trying to appease Gordon and prevent him from taking things out on his daughter.

A giant crack has appeared in the wall of the dining room; it began partway through the work on the upstairs extension – which is taking longer than expected due to the poor weather through November, and is still not close to completion. Victor has explained to her that the crack is no problem, just a bit of 'movement' during the building works that will settle soon enough, and then they can plaster over it. The building work has been going on for months and months – but she doesn't really mind. Having Victor and his little gang in has at least provided some company for her during the lonely days.

But right now this crack is ruining the image that she is creating in the dining area. She moves a large poinsettia in front of it, positioning it on a little pile of coffee table books to cover it up as much as she can. It is still visible from the side, so she removes one of the candelabra from the pair on the festive table and puts that next to the plant. It will create more space for food on the table, and divert the eye away from the crack.

But there is little hope of plastering over the cracks that have appeared in the relationship between Gordon and her, she thinks. Though she is giving it her all, he doesn't seem to understand the lengths she is going to, the hours that she spends trying to create a happy home. She wonders how much of this detail he will even notice. He is still at church – though he went to midnight mass last night as well. Christmas is the second most important time in the Christian calendar, so Sarah knows better than to be critical. But she can't escape the thought that extended Christmas services enable Gordon to spend even more time away from her and Charles – and Abby.

Like the birthday party earlier in the year, Christmas lunch is a disaster.

They are hosting Gordon's parents, Nigel and Angie, who arrived last night, tired from the long drive from North

Wales, and stayed in the Travelodge a couple of miles out of the village – knowing that it might be 'a bit much' to stay with Gordon and Sarah while the children are so young and demanding. A bit much for *them*, Sarah thinks, though they have tried to suggest that it is a magnanimous gesture on their part.

'Life is hard with a young baby and a toddler,' says Angie, soothingly, Nigel nodding in agreement. Except that everyone understands that it isn't the baby who is the demanding one. There is tension already, with Gordon set on edge at the implication that they are unable to cope with a few guests at Christmas.

'She's ruining everything. My parents won't even stay near her, for goodness' sake.'

When Abby displays only rage as a reaction to her gifts, throwing them around the room rather than playing with them, Gordon's Christmas spirit, though fortified by two church services in 12 hours, quickly dissipates.

Angie, recognising her son's displeasure, leaps in to diffuse the situation. 'What *does* she like, Sarah?' she asks, in a way that is so very grating to Sarah.

And why is it directed only at me? She thinks. Why couldn't Gordon have an answer to the question of what Abby actually likes? Why isn't it his business too? It is as if Angie is being critical of Sarah's gift choices – that is the reason she kicks off – and not of all the other underlying issues. As though she is suggesting that Sarah is entirely responsible for Abby and her behaviour, just like everyone else. *I didn't give birth to her!* She wants to scream, through gritted teeth. It has become a kind of mantra to get her through difficult situations, a way of disassociating herself from Abby's actions. Something that Gordon has been doing for a couple of years, she now realises.

By the time they sit down to the business of the Christmas meal itself, it seems that even the cutlery coordinates with the rest of the room: the atmosphere could be cut with the proverbial knife. The air is as glacial as the wintry, frost-bitten lawn just visible through the French windows.

Sarah has done her best to lighten the mood at each dark turn, but it is wearing her down to brittle edges. And all the while there is the less-than-festive accompaniment of Abby and her screeching, which is always grating, but today seems to have reached peak annoyance pitch and cuts right through her.

In another effort to do her best for Abby, and for Charles, they have been persevering with baby-led weaning ever since Charles started on solid food. Sarah has been determined that they will eat well, and be exposed to grown-up flavours whenever possible. Nutritionally, she has no doubt that this is the best way forward, but it does leave table manners somewhat lacking. She sits Abby up at the table first and then puts Charles into his high chair. At 18 months old he is now bigger than his sister, so that sitting up at the table, he looks like the older brother.

'Right; if everyone would like to seat themselves at the table, dinner is served,' Sarah announces, having set out the piles of vegetables in serving dishes in the centre of the table.

Unfortunately, through anger at not receiving her plate of festive food quickly enough, and from months of sitting by herself in the kitchen to eat rather than being up at the table with everyone else, Abby isn't in the mood for sitting quietly at the table and waiting for everyone else to be seated. She somehow finds enough of an angle from her chair to lunge at the tablecloth and pull half of the contents of the table to the floor. The earthenware dish that had belonged to Gordon's grandmother smashes against the gateleg of the table in the process, depositing roast potatoes onto the unforgiving cream-coloured rug beneath.

Angie puts her hand to her mouth in shock. 'Mum's plate!'

'What is WRONG with that child?' Gordon, who a moment ago was preparing to say Grace, is now red in the face and shouting.

He tries so hard to suppress his anger, but these days it gets the better of him more often than not, and throwing his mother's criticism into the mix isn't helping.

'Seriously! What is the matter with it?' he goes on. Sarah notices the 'it'. 'Do we not feed it, clothe it, shower every kindness on it?' He has a tendency towards Biblical constructions when particularly agitated. 'She has the very devil inside her!'

'Gordon,' his mother warns. 'I know it was Mum's plate, but that's still not a very Christian thing to say. And it is Christmas.'

And Sarah, on her knees picking potatoes and crispy shards from the long fibres of the shag pile, and wishing that she had just let Abby eat by herself in the kitchen, has also reached breaking point.

'It's not her *fault*!' she hurls back at her husband, and at her mother-in-law, automatically leaping to defend Abby in spite of feeling just as cross about her antics. 'And it's not *my* fault either.' It is Sarah's food and her fantastic festive table that has been destroyed, after all. 'And she probably *does* have the devil inside her, for all we know, the way she was conceived!'

She has thought it, but never voiced it, up until this moment. Sarah's hand now flies to her mouth. *What has she done?* There is no going back now. And Gordon has seized on her remark.

'What? What do you mean the *way* she was conceived?'

'I mean the drinking…'

'No you don't – that wasn't how she was *conceived*!'

Sarah is crying now. 'I'm sorry, Gordon. We have to be able to forgive…' and, in front of her in-laws, between sobs, still sitting on the floor in the wreckage of broken crockery, the sorry, sordid, incestuous parentage of their adopted daughter comes out. Abby whimpers in the background as Sarah is forced to tell the tale of a not-so-immaculate conception.

'The reason that poor teenage mother drank her way through the pregnancy was because she was raped. And not just that – she couldn't deal with the fact that she was raped by her own uncle. On the mother's side – her mother's own brother. I mean, it's a bloody awful story whichever way you look at it. But it's hardly Abby's fault that she's the way she is.'

There is a pause. A shocked silence reverberates around the room, punctuated only by a timely whimper from Abby.

'Merry Christmas everyone,' Sarah concludes, reaching back up to the table for her wine glass, and forgetting to care how much of that conversation its subject might have heard.

She isn't responsible for the way Abby came into the world, after all.

It is the last straw for Gordon. It is an explanation, yes. But it is also a provocation for her husband. One that violates all his righteous sense of the order of things.

'Dear Lord Christ Almighty!'

Sarah has always wondered why it is okay for Gordon essentially to blaspheme, as long as he puts a 'dear' in front of taking the Lord's name.

And she is expecting what comes next. Gordon, predictable as the sunset, always reaches straight for a Biblical quotation when he is under any kind of emotional pressure.

'I know that whoso shall receive one such little child in my name receiveth me, but help me God! What have you done to us? What have *you* brought into this house?'

Ah, yes. Me. My fault again. Of course, I should have known, thinks Sarah.

Abby's whimpers rise to a deafening screech, and she begins banging on the chair with a serving spoon, but still everyone ignores her. Charles, in contrast, sits patiently in his high chair waiting for all the fuss to die down and for someone to remember to feed him.

Angie hasn't yet closed her mouth, from the jaw that dropped open as she was listening to the tale of woe. Sarah wants to tell her to shut it, but she has caused enough trouble this afternoon. And Angie might well be struggling to process the news herself: probably not exactly the granddaughter she had been hoping for.

Sarah has seen Gordon's face angry before, but never like this.

He is mumbling to himself, now. But still quoting Matthew. 'Take heed that ye despise not one of these little ones; for I say unto you, That in Heaven their angels do always behold the face of my Father which is in Heaven.'

It doesn't make much sense given the way Gordon is reacting, but perhaps he is trying to coach himself into the correct Christian response.

Angie is still out of words; her mouth finally closed, but now set in a grim line.

'We'll leave you alone as a family to, er, work things through,' says Nigel, responding to a look that he recognises from his wife.

Sarah bridles at the clicking noises Angie makes with her tongue as she gathers up her things, perhaps intended to be soothing and placatory but having entirely the opposite effect. Sarah is left to bustle them out of the door and make all the appropriate noises and goodbyes. Gordon is good for nothing. Abby is still screeching her head off over the festive tunes Sarah has been playing quietly in the background since this morning.

Angie and Nigel beat a hasty retreat back to their Travelodge. There is a very un-Nigel like squeal of tires on the road in front of the house. It seems they can't get out of there fast enough.

Nobody has eaten a morsel of the meal that Sarah has spent days planning and hours cooking. Sarah fetches a dustpan and brush and a black bin-liner from the kitchen and makes a vague attempt to clear the carnage from the floor.

'What do you want from me?' Gordon yells, gripping onto the back of a dining chair with one hand, his other fist shaking in front of him. Sarah doesn't know if he is talking to himself or her, or the Lord. She thinks it's probably best to let the Lord answer this one, and takes another sip of wine instead and flings some red cabbage into the bin-bag.

Gordon continues to behave very strangely. He recites prayers, Bible verses, even, she thinks, hymn lyrics at one point. They accompany the noise of Abby's screeches in a weird incantation. Sarah lets him rant and ramble on. She is past caring. Somehow the noise reaches a greater crescendo, while Slade's classic announces the arrival of Christmas. But it definitely isn't merry, and everybody is certainly not having fun.

Gordon, it seems, can take it no longer. 'Jesus. I just can't do this anymore! So help me God, but I can't. Do you understand?' Again, Sarah is not quite sure whether the question is directed at her or at a higher power. But it doesn't seem to matter anyway, because he turns and walks straight out of the house without even looking at her or waiting for an answer. The sound of the front door slamming reverberates.

'Merry Christmas,' Sarah mutters again, surveying the wreckage of her feast, and of her family.

Gordon doesn't return that night, and Sarah has no idea where he is. Abandoned, Sarah spends Christmas night alone. There is no time to feel sorry for herself, though. While Charles sleeps soundly through the night as he has done from about 10 weeks old, Abby is up every hour, her restless energy murdering sleep.

VI

Gordon is gone for nearly a fortnight. In that time he makes no contact whatsoever with Sarah, who is left to manage alone with, effectively, two toddlers. Sarah learns via concerned friends that Gordon is spending time at St Bede's – a religious retreat a few miles away. She knows the place and resents the peace and quiet calm that he must be experiencing at a retreat. She feels as though she would like to retreat, herself, from some of the decisions that they have made. From life. From everything.

By the time that Gordon comes back, January has taken a bitter turn. There are a couple of inches of snow on the ground. Sarah has cleared the front pathway so that she can get the double buggy in and out. In fact, it would be fairer to say that Sarah had begun the job and, seeing her struggle, Victor had finished it. The weather has meant that the next phase of building work, a new conservatory, is temporarily on hold – but Sarah has found some comfort in knowing that Victor is close by if she needs any practical help around the house.

Gordon doesn't notice the cleared snow, or if he does, makes no comment. Instead, he is full of promises about fresh starts and resolutions. It is early in the new year. The world has been built anew. He has seen the error of his ways. He has asked God for forgiveness. He knows now what he needs to do.

'I'm going to make things right, this time. God help me, I will. I am going to do right by you and our family. After all – for richer, for poorer, in sickness and in health, to love and to cherish, till death us do part, according to God's holy law – I said it, there in that church. And I'm really going to try with Abby.'

What Sarah thinks about it all isn't really discussed. They struggle on through the next few months, but things can never be quite the same as far as Sarah is concerned. The light had already gone out of their marriage long before Gordon abandoned her at Christmas. And the hurt of that betrayal won't go away. How dare he just walk out and leave her to cope with everything. He's allowed to get away from it all for a while but she isn't? The episode is referred to as Gordon's 'epiphany'.

But Gordon's absence has enabled Sarah to have a little epiphany of her own. She is busy finding her mojo again. This year is going to be all about her. She has neglected herself and her needs for too long, something inside of her has unravelled during three years of being a stay-at-home mother. She needs some new clothes and a gym membership, she tells him. Gordon readily agrees, keen to save his marriage.

'It's time you treated yourself.'

In the depths of her heart she wonders if she is really doing it for herself, or whether the continued presence of Victor has influenced her desire to get back into shape.

In spite of his assurances to the contrary and his renewed religious fervour, Sarah feels as though she is still not able to leave Gordon alone with Abby. There is something unnerving about the way that he looks at her sometimes; truly, as though he despises her. With Charles, it is no problem. He is good with Charles. He appears to be able to manage fatherhood far better as far as his son is concerned. But he gets so angry with his daughter. Sarah notices little ways that he can be so cruel towards her at times. There are seemingly little inequalities – Abby gets criticised constantly where Charles is praised and celebrated. And Sarah knows that she can't be too critical, as she herself is guilty of treating them differently.

But somehow Abby and Gordon seem to wind each other up. Perhaps Abby does it deliberately because she can't get anything right anyway. Gordon has no patience with her. By the time she is approaching her third birthday, Abby seems to know just how to press Gordon's buttons to really make him mad. And it is all done through action, noise and gesture because Abby is still not able to talk in a really intelligible way. She prefers words to sentences, and often resorts to pointing to get what she wants. She has begun to walk now – though she was nearly two and a half before she took her first independent steps – but she is very clumsy and still falls over more than she should, or crashes into things and hurts herself.

Approaching his second birthday, Charlie is walking and talking with ease – and with far more control than his adopted big sister. His vocabulary is much bigger than Abby's, his grammatical control is far superior, his fine and gross motor skills already more finely tuned than hers. This makes Abby seem doubly clumsy whenever they are engaged in the same activity. Her clumsiness is one of the things that seems to particularly irritate Gordon. Sarah watches his upper lip curl sometimes when she crashes into something or can't complete a puzzle that her brother has finished with no trouble at all.

As they grow, seeing the two children side by side continues to accentuate everything that is wrong with Abby. Outsiders who don't know the family always assume that Charles is the older of the two siblings. He surpasses Abby on every measure at every milestone. He is at least an inch taller than his sister. Sometimes, it is almost as though they are different species, Sarah catches herself thinking.

When the work on the conservatory is complete by early summer, Sarah finds other jobs around the house that necessitate Victor's return. She likes having him around the place, enjoys their flirtatious banter, the frisson of something that they seem to share. Victor is so refreshingly different from her controlling, uptight husband. Sarah continues to push Gordon away, increasingly certain that they have no future.

The final straw comes later in the year, when Sarah catches Gordon slapping Abby for a very minor misdemeanour – she has wrenched a book from his hands, a book from which he was reading a story to Charles, and Sarah walks in just as his hand makes contact with the back of her legs.

'Gordon! Stop it! At once! You can't do that to a child! This isn't the bloody nineteen fifties! What do you think you're doing?'

'She deserved it, Sarah. She needs to be taught some lessons. You've been too soft on her. It's why she behaves the way she does. She doesn't seem to learn otherwise.'

'Oh Gordon,' Sarah says softly. 'You're the one who doesn't seem to learn.'

Sarah watches him even more closely after that, noticing how Abby is increasingly reluctant to be around him. By the following Christmas, Gordon has announced his intention to move out for an indefinite period, and schedules his departure for early in the new year. He can no longer have anything to do with Abby, he explains. He is honest with Sarah. He describes the feelings that Abby brings out in him, his desire to punish her, and the way he can find no solace in prayer.

But neither, he explains, can he live with the guilt of the decision to leave his family. Divorce is not an option. They are married in the eyes of the Lord, and always will be. He will continue to seek forgiveness and redemption.

'So I'm returning to Wales and to my parents. I am sorry, Sarah. I will let you know when I am in a better place. When I am ready to see you and Charles again.'

'But not Abby?' Sarah says.

Gordon shakes his head.

Sarah does nothing to stop him leaving. In fact, she feels very little when he makes his announcement. There is a sort of inevitability about it all. It has been a very long time since she has made any kind of effort in their relationship, herself. It has been a very long time since she cooked Gordon his favourite toad-in-the-hole supper, and even longer since they shared a good bottle of wine. She knows it is the right decision for all of them. Deep down, it is what she has wanted. She looks back on the naïve young woman of nearly four years ago, that perfectionist who was so desperate for a baby – any baby – without thought for the realities of what that might mean with a child whose needs are as deep and complex as Abby's. Sarah's life is so different from the quiet order that characterised it when they were preparing to receive Abby into their midst. Back then her biggest decisions were what household accessories to buy: whether to go for pencil-pleat or eyelet curtains, gold or silver bathroom fixtures. She had such a perfect, empty little life, even though she thought that she loved Gordon then. In her mind, they were bringing a baby into the warmest, kindest of homes. She wonders now if she ever really did love him. He never showed the crueller side of his nature until Abby came along. And though he has always been a religious man, Sarah has never really had the strength of faith that Gordon has.

Though Abby is still as difficult and demanding a child as ever, a weight of sorts lifts from Sarah at Gordon's departure. They have been in a kind of limbo for months and months. A decision feels much better than indifference. It is one less person to think about.

Gordon is kind – kind as Sarah remembers he used to be when they were first married, and very practical during the split. He believes that it is he who is as fault and therefore he wants to make the transition as straightforward as possible for Sarah. For the most part their interactions are amicable and grown-up; or perhaps it is just that they lack any emotion. The financial arrangements for childcare have been made for Charles, and some provision for Sarah so that she can stay on in the house and continue to pay the mortgage. Abby's name is noticeably absent from all their discussions and plans, though.

Once he is gone from their lives, Sarah struggles even more to cope as a single parent. With no respite whatsoever from the noise and emotional drain of caring for an out-of-control adopted child, she frequently leaves Abby to cope with her wild rages alone while she dotes on her more mild-mannered son. It is far easier that way, just to ignore it all. Some days it feels like the only way to survive. Sarah learns to shut out the noise and the demands.

And there is another unexpected development and dramatic life change ahead. Against all the odds, given the years of being unable to conceive, Sarah is pregnant once more.

Gordon is not the father.

In February, Victor moves in to the house for which he has built an extension and a conservatory and has been working on other odd jobs for the last few months.

Sarah feels that she has miraculously been given the chance for a fresh start. Life is lively with Victor: a wild adventure across rugged terrain, where it had been a gentle walk around a well-tended park with Gordon. Victor takes her out, encourages her to try new things, makes her feel as though she matters. Victor and Gordon are so different in every way, and Sarah is delighted daily by that difference.

But there is definitely no room for Abby in this new set up. Victor is willing to take on Sarah's real child as well as their own on the way, but not an adopted one.

'It's a big ask for a man, you've got to be honest. And there is something wrong with Abby, anyone can see it. She needs specialist care. Care that you can't give her,' he tells Sarah. 'Give her back. Let her go back to where she came from. It would be for the best. Why does she have to be your responsibility?'

Once that seed has been planted, it grows and spreads inside. Sarah has given Abby every chance over the years. She has, she has, over and over again, she tells herself. She has tried her best. But it was all so much of a mistake. The whole thing. It never should have been in the first place. She and Gordon should have waited a little longer for Charles to come along. But Sarah had been too impatient. She had thought that she could not have children herself. She had wanted a baby so, so badly. And then when Charles arrived it became impossible to care for two when one was so needy. Once she has articulated the thought, she knows that it is true: she no longer wants Abby, not with another baby on the way, and not if Victor doesn't want her.

Little Abimbola is rejected once more.

But it isn't quite that simple. Though the wheels are in motion now that the adoption has 'failed', it will take some time before social services are able to find a new family. It is not as easy to find a home for a four-year-old as it is for a newborn. It may take months.

Finally Sarah hears that Abby will be on the move 'soon'. It will still take a few months before it all goes through with social services – Abby will need to start school in September, so Sarah should go ahead and make those preparations – but just knowing that she will not be her responsibility any longer is enough to relieve the emotional burden. Of course, it does bring a new burden: the guilt of having to explain to Abby what is going to happen to her. Perhaps it is easier not to. A bit like telling Gordon about Abby's birth circumstances, Sarah decides to delay telling Abby. It will only cause more upset. It's kinder not to talk about it.

Sarah feels so much lighter. She can cope with Abby's tantrums and rages and her inability to be content within herself for any period of time, now that Abby is leaving and will no longer be her responsibility. There is light at the end of the tunnel. Sarah hadn't realised quite how dark it was in there now that it is ending. It is an even bigger weight being lifted from her than when Gordon left.

In the end it takes another six months before Abby is back in the care system again following her triple rejection: first by her birth-mother without even the briefest of cuddles, then by her adopted father who felt awkward even holding his child, and finally by her adopted mother, who tried so hard – but couldn't love her when her own baby came along.

By the time the transfer to a foster carer happens Abby has only just passed her fifth birthday.

But it is still too late to avoid some of the unseen damage that the last few months have brought.

Part Two:

Louise

Chapter 1

It is Friday afternoon. Lily is singing along to the radio while standing in front of the mirror and twisting strands of her hair in socks. Yes, socks. This is a 'new technique' Lily has found on YouTube and is trying out for the first time. It will, apparently, result in a head of cascading curls. Lily is a foster child currently in our care, well-settled now after nearly five years in our home.

I am more than a little sceptical about the potential of the 'new technique' to transform her long, straight locks, but there is no need to share that with Lily – she is long past paying attention to any tips I might have on hair and beauty. I am over half a century old, so what could I possibly know about fashion? Besides, it is keeping her busy and therefore giving me some precious time to think about the referral form in front of me. I frown as I scan the scant pages of the document once more.

It doesn't matter how much I read the words on the page, they don't make for comfortable reading, and I need to talk to someone about this latest referral: a little girl named Abimbola. We've invited dozens of children into our home and are regarded as experienced foster carers, which is probably one of the reasons why this has landed in my lap. This is a request for an emergency placement, which means that time is of the essence. We don't have long to make a decision. The trouble is, I have no one I can discuss it with as yet, because we have lost another one.

Supervising social worker, that is.

To lose one may be regarded as a misfortune; to lose a second looks like carelessness, as the saying goes. Dave went first; he was our very frank supervising social worker, but nearly a year ago he announced out of the blue that he was leaving social work to open a florist's shop with his wife. I suppose that plants are easier to look after than children, but we were all surprised by his decision at the time.

Now Maz is going, too.

We will miss Maz; it's a great shame she has gone. We all liked her. You feel that she is fair, and works hard for her foster carers as well as the children. The loss of Maz will be felt in all sorts of ways. Not least because she was very good at 'digging around' a referral. We have, in the past, received referrals that have left out some rather important information and she has been good at chasing that up.

If a child is coming into care for the first time and has not experienced any other foster placements, we can put missing information down to simply 'not knowing', but when a child has moved a placement – or two, or three – there is usually more to know. Why has that placement failed? What support did the child and foster carers receive to help support behaviour? Has the child had a medical and mental health assessment? Maz was good at research and asking around when there were gaps.

Sometimes a child's social worker will be so desperate to place a child that they may leave out or 'lose' important information. Not so problematic if it is straightforward and along the lines of 'this child doesn't enjoy having their hair cut', but if it is something more sinister such as 'this child threatened the carer with a knife' or 'this child has alleged rape with every carer she has lived with', then it's another matter.

If the paperwork is complete and tells you the truth then the reality, I suppose, is that you may decide not to take a placement. But, on the other hand, when you find out the hard way and experience a child's unusual or dangerous behaviour without warning, you can be sure that memories become clouded because, as far as the social worker and their manager are concerned – well, this has never happened before or it was never this bad.

So, it doesn't matter how long I keep staring at this referral for a little girl aged six years old; there are no more words on the page to explain her situation. It is very thin. It simply tells us that her adoption has 'failed', and that subsequent foster care placements have also broken down. I bridle slightly at the word 'failed', which makes it sound somehow like it was the child's fault. It's the first thing that makes me think that this girl deserves a chance.

In the absence of a supervising social worker I have put the word out locally to see if anyone knows anything about this case. And still our jungle drum doesn't beat. Like any other group, foster carers create their own communities independent of the agency or authority they work for; communities which inform and protect each other. When you're new to fostering and have not joined these networks you are more likely to fall prey to the kind of redactions on Abimbola's file. That's obviously not the case for us though, so it's unusual not to hear anything back. We have no information whatsoever, with no Maz to do the difficult digging, but there is another, significant reason why I am not hearing anything on the grapevine: Abimbola – pretty name, sounds African – has come from out of county, actually from the other end of the country. That means that either her family moved here and she suddenly went into care or perhaps she has been moved for protection, or she has been moved because – well, there are other reasons we may just be about to find out.

So I *really* want to talk this one over with Maz.

Maz was very professional and did not give away too much in the end before announcing her resignation, but we guess that she was not over impressed with her manager and the culture in her office. Her manager used to work in South Africa and was well known amongst the fostering community. She was known as the 'Queen of the Bad Decision'. I know a number of good foster carers who left because she used intimidation and bullying on foster carers – and even some of the children, particularly teenagers, whom she seemed to despise.

But every cloud has a silver lining, and just after we learnt about Maz's departure, we found out that her manager had moved on too: the Queen of the Bad Decision has left to become an IRO – an independent reviewing officer. It's an important role – they are considered to be the independent voice of the child. (Though we often smile if children's social services use the term 'independent' when they all share the same coffee cups.)

So now we have to wait to see who we get next, but a change in two layers of personnel may bode well for us in the long term. I am optimistic.

In the meantime, Lily, (still singing, still merrily sock-plaiting) has held onto her social worker for over a year now, which is not bad – especially as this one is a locum. Of course, given all the various instabilities in their lives, the attachment and importance a child can invest into a social worker can be huge; so when they announce that they are leaving, the impact on the child also has the potential to be enormous, especially when you factor in all the loss that a child may have already been through. Having many social workers can compound the fractures in an already fragile heart. But Lily has maintained some consistency of late, and that is good.

But it doesn't help me with the decision about Abimbola. Right now I need an honest and frank discussion and we are in limbo – I literally have no one to contact.

The trouble is, me being me, I am already mentally locating the African masks we have in the attic from a long-ago safari in the years before children came along, thinking that perhaps something like this might make Abimbola feel more at home. I know I've got some fabric somewhere with a vibrant African print; I can use it as a throw over the sofa – that might be nice and welcoming. There are some animal-print blankets, folded up in a box somewhere. I could dig those out, too. All my white, middle-class preconceptions and prejudices are stacking up beautifully, all based on the name I have seen written down in her file: Abimbola. By now I have done a quick internet search. The name is West African – most popular in Benin or Nigeria. It's a name that means 'born with wealth'. Well, they couldn't have got that more wrong, could they – at least in terms of emotional wealth, looking at her file.

Under 'Ethnicity' the box says 'N/A'. Not Applicable. That makes me laugh. How can it not be applicable? Well, I know how. We aren't terribly ethnically diverse in our sheltered part of south-west England, so children from different ethnicities are more difficult to place. I expect the powers that be think that by glossing over ethnicity they have a better chance of finding at least a temporary home for a child. And I will want to make her feel as at home as

I possibly can. I think about Lily and her YouTube-sourced sock-created curls and wonder if I should get her searching for tutorials on styling afro hair. With limited time to prepare and an ignorance of her cultural heritage, it is the best I can do. I even think about turning the heating up, then remind myself that she has obviously lived in England for most of her short life. All these thoughts tell me that, actually, in my mind, I suppose I have already said 'yes'. The thought of a six-year-old child repeatedly rejected and left with nowhere to go – which must surely be the case if she is coming from so far away – tugs at the heartstrings. I can't really say 'no', even though I have plenty of reservations. It goes against my very nature to leave a child stranded in the care system.

Although in truth, I have to keep reminding myself that this is not my decision to make alone. No woman is an island, and I have the rest of my family to consider. As with all referrals, we must run it by the children first and gauge whether they will be supportive or not, and who they might be happy to tolerate living in their home. (I also need to factor into this process their age and mood. A teenage girl once stayed for three months and Vincent, my eldest birth son, who was then aged eight years, said he had had enough of girls and never wanted foster children here again. I think he's over that now.) I'd like to discuss it with everyone together, but Lily is obviously a little preoccupied with the hair-sock thing, Vincent is out at rugby training and Jackson is playing a hockey match, so that discussion will have to wait at least a little longer, too.

I check her date of birth. The poor thing has only just turned six. It was her birthday only two days ago. I wonder how she spent it. Emergency care wouldn't be my first choice of location for a birthday celebration. I wonder if it was even marked in any way. Abimbola probably wasn't aware of the date. Perhaps we should have a little party when she gets here. I could bake a cake. See, I'm doing it again – getting ahead of myself and already mentally picturing a little girl of colour in my kitchen blowing out six candles.

Then I turn the page (there aren't many of them) and note with some trepidation that Abimbola has been in four different foster placements in the 10 months she has been in care. Experience has taught me to read these notes carefully. I take them one by one, trying to read between the lines of each. The first placement was temporary – but so are most foster placements, such is the nature of fostering – so that's that one, and I won't read too much into it. The second placement report says that Abimbola didn't get on with the other children. Hmm. I don't like the sound of that too much. Was that Abimbola? Or did the other children not like and accept her? It isn't clear. That might need a little bit more unpicking. If only there was someone to ask! The third placement was temporary and the foster carers retired. Talk about timing! I wonder if they retired, or left? Why would you take on a child and then retire during the placement itself?

The fourth placement is the one that really bothers me, coming on the heels of the other three. The fourth placement 'broke down' because the foster carers were 'inexperienced' and could not manage her behaviour. Alarm bells always ring when I hear that a placement has broken down. Again, there isn't enough narrative here to help me see what went wrong. 'Inexperienced' is a lovely euphemism that might cover anything. Was it just because they were new and were not prepared to deal with all the hurt a little girl could display from being rejected? Did the carers not get the support they needed? Or was there something more sinister about Abimbola's behaviour that isn't being said? I take a referral with a pinch of salt and a healthy dose of inference. The information can be months, or in some cases even years, out of date. And clever use of language can hide the truth sometimes. A phrase such as 'lively and energetic' might well in reality mean 'won't shut up or sit still', and 'has a little way to go with table manners' is, in fact, code for 'attacks food like a rabid dog'.

One of the most difficult aspects of a new placement is that rarely do we get the opportunity to meet the child first so that both sides can get a feeling about each other. A child coming straight from court or via the police will not have any time or opportunity to come for tea and sleepovers and begin a process that might help ease them into our home. A child coming from another placement *may* have time to come for tea if you can arrange it amongst yourselves, but I have learnt not to expect the social worker to have time or the inclination to organise this. Instead, a child is very often simply delivered to the doorstep and then, after the briefest of introductions, everyone is left to get on with it.

The last foster carers for Abimbola might have handed in the dreaded '28-day notice' for any number of reasons, though most often it is a simple one: they have not been supported to manage the child's behaviour.

I realise that may sound like I am suggesting that some foster carers aren't very good; I'm not. But it is worth remembering that most foster carers are regular people just wanting to help out and do a good deed for the community and for social cohesion. The trouble is that these days children coming into care are not nearly as straightforward as they used to be. They may need specialist help and support, and instead are bumped around a system that hasn't got the time or resources to help them as they deserve – and that can bring a range of frighteningly challenging behaviours with it.

The only other things to note on the form after the inadequate chronology of care are the unfilled, or at best sparsely filled boxes. 'Physical Description' is blank – but perhaps can be explained along the same lines as the equally insulting 'N/A' that was in the ethnicity section. There is a short paragraph in the 'Child's Personality' space on the form: *Abimbola enjoys adult interaction and attention. She likes to be cuddled and likes to smile and giggle with those care givers around her. Abimbola is a very loving child, who thrives on the attention of adults.* All well and good, but doesn't tell me too much about what she is really like as a person. For 'Likes and Dislikes' I learn that she 'enjoys playing outdoors.' Right. Again, not a terrific amount to go on. 'Self-Care Skills' is blank. Does that mean she doesn't have any? Or simply that the form hasn't been filled in very well? There is an emotional and behavioural section which includes the words 'occasional tantrums'. I suspect that they are not occasional, and perhaps 'tantrum' may be a euphemism. After all, we are talking about a child who must be struggling to coexist with the wounds of rejection.

But none of this is helping me to make up my mind about Abimbola. The one other thing I do know is that a few of my fellow foster carers have also received this same referral – and passed. That doesn't bode well either – but perhaps they are wary for the same reasons I am: the total absence of any useful information about her background and why she is in this situation.

I have, of course, already begun to talk this through with my husband, Lloyd, this morning before he disappeared into his study for work. Like me, he is in the happy position of being able to work from home – though hours can be odd. He is a graphic designer, and having clients all over the world in different time zones is a factor that can sometimes dictate his working hours: he might have to make himself available at strange times of the day. He has a conference call with a client this morning and doesn't want to be disturbed for a couple of hours. Usually I would go and have these conversations aloud with him, but all this is running around my head unfiltered and undiluted. I know that from what he said first thing, Lloyd isn't sure about this one either – he shares my reservations – and the anxiety we both feel is compounded by this business of not having a new supervising social worker to guide us.

What we *have* had, though, is several calls from the placements team, who are sounding increasingly desperate with each conversation. The child's social worker has also said that she is willing to come to our house for a meeting and talk to us about her – from the other end of the country – if it will help us to decide.

That suggests a great deal of commitment, but does it also suggest that there is a complexity to Abimbola's situation that needs to be discussed in person? I'm not sure. If only I could talk to Maz. Or anyone, in fact. Right now I'd even take five minutes with the Queen of the Bad Decision. At least it would be another perspective.

When Lloyd breaks for coffee later in the afternoon, he gets bombarded by the outpouring of all my conflicting thoughts. He is a good man and generally thinks well of most people. Unlike me – after all my experiences of children's social care (firstly as a looked-after child myself, and secondly as a seasoned foster carer), I have a tendency to look at things differently, more critically and often more catastrophically. But I am married and part of that commitment means meeting half-way.

My gut says, 'Yes, come here and meet us!' I tell him.

But Lloyd, more pragmatically, takes another view. 'That's a very long way to travel, and expensive. Why don't you both talk on the phone?' He hands me a coffee and stirs his own. 'Hmmm.'

When I'm meeting someone for the first time I prefer not to talk on the phone, for the obvious reason that it's easier to gauge a person if they have to look at you. It makes it much easier to read them. And anyway, I have a secret weapon: Dotty. Dotty is a Chihuahua-Jack Russell cross. We have two of them, actually: Douglas is Dotty's Jackawowa partner in crime, though he seems to have more of the Chihuahua temperament, but they are both little dogs with big characters. Dotty is definitely more Jack Russell and I just have to watch her reaction to any newcomer to find out whether they are on the level or not. She is so good at judging people that I wonder why MI5 don't use Jackawowas to infiltrate spy rings. But Lloyd is right. In this instance, a telephone conversation makes much more practical sense. He raises his eyebrows in an expression that I take to mean 'go on then', and so I get dialling. He stays in the kitchen with me. Conference call over, the page layouts he is designing can wait for a few more minutes.

'It's a sad story,' Abimbola's social worker, who introduces herself as Annie, explains to me. 'She was adopted as a newborn baby, but the adoptive parents had another child shortly afterwards – and then separated not long after that; there is some suggestion of neglect.'

Oh, so she and the adoptive dad had a baby *after* adopting Abimbola. That's interesting.

'Then, once the adoptive parents split, mum met someone else fairly quickly. Mum and new dad decided that Abimbola didn't work in their new family unit.'

I can't help it. I begin mentally judging people I have never met, as the social worker adds, 'Because mum was having *another* baby.'

I sit and listen to this tale of woe, seething inside. 'Right, so this first child no longer suited them?'

As a child who was fostered and adopted myself, I know only too well that the 'brought in' child can go to the bottom of the pile. I think I know how this story goes. If the family were on a boat that was sinking and a small raft pulled up, which child would the parents grab first to put on the raft? It's not too difficult to work out the answer. I know that when I was a child I felt pretty certain that the blood went first.

'Exactly.'

I am horrified that the social worker and the authorities who arranged her adoption in the first place allowed her to be passed over like a dog to be rehomed.

Perhaps I let my own memories and feelings get involved, but even before I have finished the conversation with Annie, I think I have decided to support this little girl. Rejection, rejection, rejection. I feel so sad and cross that this poor little one has been pushed to the back of everyone's priorities. One more question, though.

'I can't see anything about her actual birth family on the form. Do you know anything about who her mother and father were?'

'Nothing much at all. It was a teenage pregnancy. Abimbola was put up for adoption straight away.'

I wonder if her birth parents know what's happened to her. What a nexus of events.

Though I have made no promises, and merely offered to phone the social worker back later on this evening, Lloyd – who knows me too well – watches me put the phone down and asks with a resigned sigh, 'So, when's she coming?'

'I think the social worker would have driven her there and then!'

Even though we still haven't said a definite 'yes', when Lloyd returns to his study, I set the wheels in motion to find a school that will take her. My next three phone calls are to the local primaries to ask if they have any spaces. Children in care are a priority in the education system – which is only right and proper given that they aren't much of a priority anywhere else. Headteachers have to have a pretty good excuse for why a child can't come to their school, so I feel confident that something can be arranged. I also drive down to the surgery to collect the forms from our GP to register Abimbola there.

Later that night I relay my conversations and the progress I have made through the afternoon back to Annie. She can take up the reins now and sort out the rest of the admissions procedure. I can let her do the school's bidding and make the arrangements. Although she is pressing for me to make it sooner, I request next Monday for Abimbola's arrival in order to give us time to arrange her room and prepare the children. I need my gang to be supportive of what I suspect will be in an interesting next chapter in our lives.

I have no way of knowing quite what Abimbola will be arriving with in terms of clothing, so on Saturday morning I head to the shops and buy a set of pyjamas and some trousers and tops, but I'm guessing because I don't know her height or size. I think Nigerians are small, though, so I err a little bit on the side of caution and go for things in the 5-6 years range. She's only just six, after all.

Each member of the family starts preparing in their own ways. Lily finds time away from the bathroom hair salon over the weekend (as I suspected, the promised curls didn't materialise, but she has plans to experiment more with the sock technique) in order to make a lovely welcome card, though it takes two goes to get the spelling of 'Abimbola' right. Jackson and Vincent donate a small toy each to leave on her shelf. I make the trip to the loft to find those masks and other bits and pieces from our travels. I find everything colourful that I can, any fabric or blanket that has a bold design that might resemble an African print. I investigate Nigerian food and cooking and stock up on rice. None of the supermarkets near me stock yams, though. Even Waitrose lets me down. So, aside from the problem of the yam shortage, we are ready. As ready as we can be.

And yet, the whole time, I can't shake the feeling that something isn't right.

Abimbola is only young, but is being removed from her whole family and extended family, the town and places that she is familiar with, and being transported right to the other end of the country. Why? It seems very drastic. There has to be a really good reason, and I haven't heard it yet. What are we getting ourselves into?

And not every placement goes as you hope. What happens to Abimbola if it doesn't work out with us?

Chapter 2

I feel an immense pressure on us, my family, to make this work. Of course, as foster carers we always do try and make it work – but sometimes it just doesn't. I would have been happier if at least we could have met Abimbola first, and she could have met us. But this little girl is being driven – by a social worker she barely knows – for miles and miles from one end of the country to another. I am still puzzled by this: are there no foster carers in her area that could have taken her? Or at least in a district a little bit closer?

I know that numbers are dwindling. Fewer people want to become foster carers because it is hard, and you receive next to nothing for your efforts. I wish they would change fostering and make it a career: a proper job so that foster carers could receive a minimum wage. There must be all sorts of ways to attract more foster carers; but to not have *any* in Abimbola's area is just strange.

My greatest concern is, simply, what if this doesn't work out? They are moving this child across the country, and I feel responsible for that. She knows no one. I lack confidence in the details of the referral. Experience has taught us that what is *not* said is usually what we need to know the most, and I feel like there is much that has been left unsaid.

Monday comes.

I have everything ready. The children are as prepared as they can be. But I do still have an uncomfortable feeling that won't leave me. When I spoke to Annie, she said that the last carers were inexperienced and 'could not cope' with Abimbola's behaviour. The primary caregiver was a woman who was at home alone with the girl whilst her husband was out of the house. This primary carer had locked herself in the bathroom because she was scared of Abimbola when she had refused to go to bed and had spat in her face. But this is a six-year old girl. How scared can you be by a little child barely out of reception class? To new foster carers I suppose this could be distressing – but if they had been trained properly they would know it is rare that happy, well-adjusted children go into care.

Most children in care have experienced trauma.

Many have seen things that the rest of us could not imagine.

And it takes a while to learn how to empathise rather than judge. Children coming into my house have spat at me before, kicked me and told me that they hate me. Even my own children have done this, at some stage. How much more complex it must be for a damaged child without a secure attachment history being thrust into new home after new home.

Experience has taught me this truth: all behaviour is communication, and when a child is telling us something, we just need to listen.

Lloyd is in his studio. He made an effort to get ahead of the week by doing some work on Sunday so that he could help meet and greet our ward and the social worker. I am pretending to do things, when really I am pacing about, looking out of the window every couple of minutes.

I have my usual food at the ready for all occasions and eaters. It's a long, long journey. Abimbola may have been carsick. They may not have stopped for refreshments for a while. Or she might be just fine. I don't know. Many of our social workers tend to take children to McDonald's. Other burger restaurants are available. I suppose the thinking is that it's a treat, something that a child can relate to. Knowing children as I do, and especially those in care, they are usually pretty familiar with the Big Mac and may prefer something else, something a little more nutritional.

Have a look next time you are in one of those family restaurant chains. When I have taken my children to McDonald's, perhaps as a treat when we go bowling or to the cinema, it is easy to spot a social worker with the looked-after child. Sometimes they appear along with the dads who have access. It's as though fast food restaurants have become a holding place for damaged and disenfranchised children.

Somehow I have made it through the morning. Abimbola's arrival time was always a moveable feast: given the amount of motorway they are covering, timing was approximate. I know that they were planning to set out early this morning. Lloyd and I have some soup for lunch. I am just cleaning the bowls and putting them away when the doorbell goes.

This is it!

I take care to make sure that I have put our two dogs in the sitting room. I had told the social worker over the phone that we have two dogs and a cat; she said Abimbola was fine with animals, but you can't be too careful and they can be overwhelming when visitors first arrive.

I open the door to a larger lady, somewhere in her thirties, with long shoulder-length hair died a sort of henna red. She is wearing a lot of blue and purple. Colour always strikes me first. She is so wide that I can't see Abimbola at first. I smile and say hello.

Standing behind her is a little scrap of a girl. She looks directly at me.

'But she's not...' I trail off. 'Black', I go to say, but stop myself. She has pale grey eyes and white, white skin. Almost too white skin. Any trace of the African child I have mentally constructed bears no relation to the tiny little girl standing in front of me.

'... as tall as I expected,' I rescue, lamely.

So, the African heritage, if it exists, is hidden. What is not well hidden is a look that I recognise only too well, and one that fills me with concern.

Her face is flat; strikingly so.

I have seen this before on children we have looked after who have had foetal alcohol damage or drug abuse damage.

I take a deep breath. This is *not* what I was expecting – on so many levels. We have worked with these children before. It was hard work. Very hard work.

Straight away I look at Lloyd and know that he shares my trepidation. We are too familiar with the behaviours of these children to embrace this unknown quantity. Why didn't they tell us before? It has never been a good mix for us to have a child with these conditions in with our other children. Some of the comments on the referral are starting to make sense now.

I recognise the symptoms immediately, and I have no medical training. Why is there nothing in her notes about something that should be instantly recognisable? What I see is a head that is too small. The smooth, wide ridge between her nose and upper lip, like a pastry-fold, has been forgotten. Her eyes are small and far apart, and she is too small for her age, more like the size of a toddler than a child of five. The pyjamas and clothes I have bought will be too big. Though that is the least of our worries.

If I am correct in my diagnosis, and I think that there is no mistaking it, then there will have been untold damage to her brain and internal organs.

I am going to have to tread carefully with the social worker who, if experienced, will also know, without doubt, that Abimbola has foetal alcohol syndrome, or FAS.

'Hi… Annie,' I say, using the name of the social worker that I have been speaking to on the phone, although in my head she sounded older than the woman who stands before me.

'Actually, it's Kate.'

Ok, so not Annie, the one I was speaking to on the phone. What is going on?

This social worker – Kate – moves aside so that Abimbola can come into the house. Our new 'emergency placement' takes a step across the threshold. She does not 'tread carefully', but trips over the step and crashes into the wall, knocking the umbrella stand over – that Lloyd reaches for in a flash, and saves, in a deft movement the like of which I haven't seen since his days of squash-playing.

I invite them all into the kitchen whilst carefully watching this little girl's movements. It is plain to see that she has poor co-ordination skills as she negotiates her way clumsily around the kitchen table and chairs.

I offer Kate a drink. She wants coffee, and when I put some biscuits on the plate she doesn't hold back.

I am waiting for her to introduce us to our new guest. And I have already made up my mind that I need this to be very definitely a 'guest'. This needs to be a temporary arrangement. I am already feeling overwhelmed by the work ahead of us. She doesn't say anything, so I do.

'Hello Abimbola. It's very lovely to meet you.'

She looks back at me and smiles. Then makes a strange rattle-giggle sound. Have I said her name wrong?

Like Kate, Abimbola then gets straight into helping herself to the biscuits.

'Did you have any lunch?' I say, to break through the sound of two sets of teeth chomping on chocolate chip cookies.

'No,' Kate says, 'we didn't. I drove straight here. And I have to get back before it gets dark. I'm not good at driving out of the area in the dark. So I won't take up too much of your time.'

I ask if she has time for a sandwich. Kate nods enthusiastically – as does Abimbola. She is very pasty, and so thin that I can see the pattern of blue veins in her face and neck. My mothering instinct kicks in. Whatever else she needs, and I sense that her needs are great, right now this girl needs feeding. I set about making cheese and ham sandwiches and add a packet of crisps for Abimbola. I notice Kate's slightly crestfallen face and offer her a packet too.

Lloyd politely talks to Kate about her journey. It has taken the best part of six hours to get here.

'Her stuff is still in the car. I'll grab it.'

Lloyd follows her outside to help. I keep a keen eye on Abimbola, watching her eat, which she does with her mouth wide open, masticating so that we can see bread soggying up in her mouth. I am already evaluating all the work we need to do. This will be a good place to start. Not right this second, but soon, because I am quite a stickler for table manners. I think these details are important and help children when they become adults to smooth their way through the world. I feel already that nobody has invested in her, although she was adopted – and the assumption with adoption is that the family do the work because they want this child and have often been through quite a tough process to get her. Again, I ask myself what is going on.

My mind is churning. I wonder if Lloyd has had the foresight to ask about Abimbola's suspected FAS while he is alone with Kate. I don't want to do that in front of Abimbola, of course; that would not be appropriate.

When Lloyd returns with just a black plastic bin liner half full of clothes and a broken scooter, we raise our eyebrows at one another. The scooter is clearly too tall for her, and we have several in the shed that are much better than this. I ask if she had any possessions from her adoptive family: any photos, keepsakes.

Kate shakes her head. 'No, but the last foster carer took some pictures of her whilst out on a family walk.' She roots around inside the bin bag and pulls out a picture frame with a photograph of a large group of adults and little Abimbola in the front. I feel sad for her. The image shows that she doesn't belong, somehow, and was clearly just passing through. I wonder if she even knows who they are?

When both Abimbola and Kate have eaten their sandwiches swilled down with a glass of apple juice, I suggest that Lloyd shows Abimbola her room. Lloyd knows what I am about and responds to his cue.

'Good idea, Louise. I'm sure that's exactly what Abimbola would like, isn't it? It's a lovely room. Let's go and see…'

Kate gets up as if to follow, too.

Oh no, you're not getting off that lightly, I think to myself.

Out loud I say, 'Oh, it's okay, Kate. I will show you round too in a bit; I just need to ask you some questions.'

She brings out her file and the usual documents for signing. She hands me the delegated authority form, which looks like I can do just about everything: dentists, doctors, hairdressers and so on.

I ask her a straight question. 'Has Abimbola had a full paediatric review?'

Her head is buried in her bag as she gives her reply. 'Not as far as I know, no.'

So, I say to her, 'Do you think she has foetal drug or alcohol syndrome?'

'Oh, I don't think so. She looks fine.'

I notice that she is still busying herself with what appears to be something imaginary in her bag and making a point of not looking at me. I ask to see Abimbola's education review. 'Annie promised that it would be emailed over but I haven't had it yet.'

Kate says, without checking, 'Oh, I don't seem to have that. I will make a note to send it to you.'

I ask her if she has any information about the birth parents.

'No, nothing on the files we have.' She adds, 'But I think she did move counties a couple of years ago when her adoptive parents split up.'

'Shouldn't that paperwork follow the child?' I ask.

Kate shrugs her shoulders. It doesn't take me long to realise that I am not going to get much out of Kate. She either doesn't know – or has been told not to tell us – the answers. We have fostered for nearly a decade now and in that time we have seen all sorts of shenanigans when it comes to children's social services. My experience has taught me that social workers can be a little like people who drink too much, and when they go to the doctor's and are asked how many units they consume each week, answer '13.8' – in other words, just below the recommended limit of 14. I am being fobbed off here, for sure.

Information about the birth families and the agencies surrounding the child should be there in the paperwork. It should be kept in order – if not for us then for the child, in case they ever request to see it later in life. Missing paperwork is a bad sign. And Kate's evasive behaviour is doing little to help – in fact, it is feeding my suspicions.

I try one last question. 'Her name – Abimbola. It's, well, it's rather unusual. Do you know anything about that?'

'Oh – is *that* how you say it? Yes, it's a bit different, isn't it? We have just been calling her Abby. I think she prefers that.'

Lloyd walks back into the kitchen with Abimbola-Abby, who is holding on to Lloyd's hand and smiling.

It sounds sweet, that image. Except that this little girl doesn't know us yet. I am watchful to see if the child has attachment issues. Knowing what little I do about her history so far, it wouldn't surprise me at all if she has some kind of insecure attachment. A concern for carers is that a child might potentially go off with anyone who speaks to them or is nice to them. I have watched my birth children – who grew up with a secure base, mainly, with both of us watching over them and protecting them – seem awkward around people they did not know. They would have kept looking at me or Lloyd if invited to go off with a stranger to look at something. They probably would have stood next to us, something familiar. This young girl is happy to wander off with a strange man in a strange house and hold his hand as though it is the most normal thing in all the world. I don't like it one little bit.

Lloyd and I sit at the table and sign the relevant paperwork. What else are we to do? Hand her back? My alarm bells are ringing loud and clear, but here is a little girl who has been taken from everything and everyone she knows to stay with us. It's not her fault. Our job is to do the best we can for her.

I ask who I contact if I have any concerns about Abimbola. I have constructed such a definite picture of a little black girl in my head that even with the evidence before my eyes it is going to take me a while to get used to calling her 'Abby'.

'A regional social worker has been selected to pick up her case and they will be in touch soon,' she says, airily.

I offer a tight-lipped smile. Internally I am screaming. This is my worst-case scenario: no children's social worker and no supervising social worker.

When Kate has gone I will be making some phone calls and sending off some sternly-worded emails. It probably won't do much good, but it will make me feel better.

Meanwhile, I realise that I have left the dogs shut in the sitting room the whole time. Kate wasn't fussed about seeing Abby with them, and now I can hear them yapping. I can practically feel Dotty's desperation to get to Abby and check her out under the guise of saying hello. I have a feeling that she won't like Kate very much, and will simply keep on barking – this is one occasion when I don't think I even need Dotty's powers of making it very clear when she thinks that someone is not sincere. I have worked that one out for myself in this case.

There is so much more to say, but also nothing more that I am going to get from Kate. She is all that I have, though, so as she stands to leave I ask for her business card. I want her number.

'I've written contact numbers down in the paperwork,' she insists.

She makes a break for the front door and once there, seems in a rush to get back into her car. Abby doesn't seem terribly interested or upset by the fact that Kate is leaving, but does stand at the door and wave when Lloyd asks her if she would like to say goodbye.

The car pulls away, and off she goes back to wherever she came from.

And here we are, left with a young child with potentially tons of problems, a bin bag, a broken scooter several sizes too large and a social worker who couldn't leave fast enough. I look at Lloyd, and can tell he feels as I do. I start collecting up the African print blankets that are draped over every chair. Our collective mood is flat. Normally there is a buzz around a new child coming to stay, but not today.

Abby catches sight of one of the masks, something I picked up on holiday in my twenties and scoops it up, placing her fingers in the eyeholes. She seems fascinated by it.

'It's a mask. Look here, you can make a new face, like this; see,' I say, and hold it up in front of my face. She takes it back in her hands and holds it up in front of her own face. It looks really sinister: a grandly terrifying ceremonial mask on this tiny body. For some reason I can't explain it makes me shudder and I take it back from her straight away. 'But it's not really a toy, so we'll just put it over here for now.'

Lloyd eyes the scooter again and heads out to the shed. He returns with three of the other scooters, bringing them to the back door.

He calls her over. 'Right, then, Abimbola. Let's see which one is the best size for you!'

'I think she likes to be called "Abby", I say, looking directly at her. No response, other than to leap towards the scooters. Naming is so important, and she doesn't seem to care what we are calling her. She is engrossed in the scooters, though, and happily tests all of them. The right one is Vincent's old lime-green wheeled scooter. He is not here to ask, but hopefully he won't mind if Abby borrows it. I think it may do her good to whizz about for a bit after being cooped up all that way on a long car journey with all those thoughts going round in her head.

Poor child. She gets on the scooter and tears around the lawn: round and round in circles, standing, stunting, one leg in the air, laughing and generally looking like she is the happiest little girl in the world.

She is in a strange setting, with strange people, away from all she knows.

This, too, is not right.

Chapter 3

Abby has been whizzing round the garden for over an hour, now.

What were those words on her referral form? They weren't wrong about her liking to play outdoors.

She looks very happy. She is chatting away to herself. I'm not quite sure what she is saying, but the conversation keeps her engaged. I watch through the kitchen window for a while, wondering where all that energy is coming from. I don't like to interrupt, but it's time I introduced her to Dotty and Doug. I call Abby in to say hello to them.

I open the sitting room door and out fly the dogs, so excited after their incarceration that they tumble around in a blur of fur. First they come and say hello to me and run round the kitchen. Then they run up to Abby, both dogs giving her the full sniff and tail waggle treatment. She passes: they love her. She flops down onto the floor while they jump on her; she is not scared at all. Rather, she is in fits of giggles.

I tell both dogs to get off her. Doug does so straight away, being slightly more obedient and controllable, but Dotty wants to wash Abby and be her doggie mummy, it seems. I suggest she runs out in the garden with them. She charges round the garden: up every path and corner and back again. She has explored the entire garden within minutes. We have a fairly big garden, but she makes it seem small. She is all over it, able to cover a huge amount of space in seconds – with the dogs behaving like it's the first time they have ever been in the garden.

I bring her out a plastic cup of squash and another biscuit. Living on a hill means that the garden has several levels to it. She sits down on the garden step that divides the top from the bottom garden and both dogs sit tight next to her. Their eyes follow the biscuits into her mouth. That's when I first properly notice her teeth. They are huge, like tomb stones, far too big for her face; and the whole effect is emphasised by her head being too small. All part of the FAS.

Quickly she is back up and on the scooter again, now with both dogs tagging behind. She seems to be deep into an imaginary game. I hang back in the garden and pretend to do some weeding while I listen carefully to what she says.

'Come on, guys, let's go get her. Let's rescue Abby.'

Ok, so she does call herself Abby, rather than Abimbola. But why is she talking about herself in the third person, and why does she need rescuing?

I let her carry on circling the garden on scooter and on foot; she makes me a little nervous as she leaps off the steps and climbs up onto the stone garden walls that separate off the barbecue area. She jumps with no regard for her landing. She is not just a tomboy, she seems to have no sense of her own self and safety. My own children would have been far more cautious, at least checking out that it was safe to land.

Now that she has flown off the wall a few times and the novelty of a near-death experience seems to have worn off, she has found a stick and is using it as some kind of a weapon.

I keep watching her, fascinated. I took my sons out for so many walks in woods and country gardens when they were her age. They loved finding sticks to bash a big tree with or use as a gun, or even just to carry around as a kind of staff. But Abby seems very aggressive with it. I hang by, still finding imaginary weeds – well, not so imaginary, there are plenty of them but I am not really concentrating on the garden – just in case she attempts to hurt the dogs. My fears are unfounded: she does not.

What she is doing is battling an imaginary enemy who is hurting 'other Abby'. I wonder if 'other Abby' is herself, and she is acting out saving herself. The thought that a child might feel the need to play this out seems sad, but I think that I am learning a little about our new guest.

It occurs to me that Kate, the not terribly sociable social worker, didn't even take a quick glimpse at Abby's room. I'm surprised. I could be sticking the child in a cupboard, for all she knows. I definitely got the impression that she just wanted to go with as little fuss as possible to avoid driving in the dark – no matter that this is a child's wellbeing that we are talking about. I ask Lloyd to keep an eye on Abby while I take the bin bag up to her room. As I walk up the stairs, I am leaking clothes – there is a tear in one side of the plastic. Not even an intact bin bag, then. I look at the trail of clothes that now litter the stairway and am whipped up into a fury once again, which increases with each item I gather up.

None of these clothes are new or her size. She is a tiny six-year-old. The clothes are old fashioned, look as though they have been foraged from a jumble sale, and might fit the average 10-year-old. They are clean, at least: I can smell the laundry detergent, but she basically has no clothes. It is a good job I bought a few bits over the weekend to keep us going. They are also too big, but not as ridiculous as this little collection.

We have a week until Abby starts school. Annie, the 'phone' social worker, has managed to get Abby into a local school – not the same one as my other children, which would have been handy, but at least the place is sorted. This time next week I will be having to get two lots of children to two places at the same time. Ah well, it won't be the first time I have had to be in two places at once. We'll give it a go and work it out somehow.

Meanwhile I put the one photo of Abby's life that Kate (who I am mentally referring to as the 'chauffeur' social worker) showed me onto the chest of drawers. Otherwise, Abby has nothing. It doesn't seem much to help her try to feel at home. There are no toys (apart from the broken scooter quickly substituted), no comfort blanket, no teddies. Just some rubbish clothes that seem almost to have been picked at random, and the photo. This girl was born, adopted, and fostered four times, and now, here with us, all she has to show for her little life is a ripped bin liner full of useless clothes. Poor kid.

I keep a present cupboard on the landing. It's an old airing cupboard, not big enough now for our household linen – which is carefully stored in a built-in cupboard on the other side of the hall and happens to be one of my favourite places in the world. An odd thing to say, I know, but the big wide-slatted shelves hold my carefully laundered ironed and folded bed linen and towels, and it gives me great comfort. I love the feeling this cupboard gives me when I open it and see the stacks of folded sheets, pillow cases and duvet covers with bars of scented soap buried amongst them. I inhale a deep breath of order and peace of mind, and the world feels good.

The old airing cupboard is full of potential items of use for foster children and presents for other children's birthdays. More often than not they have been bought in sales and when I happen to see things that I think might come in useful. There are also several rolls of wrapping paper, different sized dispensers of sellotape, and a collection of cards for boys and girls of various ages. There are three teddy bears in boxes nestling in there, unused and waiting for an owner.

If I make a child aware of the cupboard they might start helping themselves, so best to keep temptation away until boundaries are learnt. If I let Abby choose, she might not be able to cope with it, looking at her meagre possessions to date, so I make the choice for her. I transport myself back to being a six-year-old girl and think what she would have chosen. I pick up the two-tone brown fluffy rabbit. It's soft and eye-wateringly cute. I put the rabbit in its box on Abby's bed. I think it's important that she knows the toy is new, just for her. Often foster children get cast-offs – which is fine; my own children have had plenty of hand-me-downs and I was always grateful. Well, nearly always – I was horrified once when a relative gave us a dirty old car seat, that looked as though it might have survived several crashes. As soon as they left I put it in the community skip. There's pre-loved and there's insulting. A healthy mix of cast-offs from the charity shop when the children want to spend their pocket money is fine. But something new when you aren't used to having it? That's special. I love watching foster children opening shiny new gifts. It's a statement of their worth, and a step towards them understanding their self-worth.

I head downstairs to the kitchen to begin to get ready for the return of the other children. I have recently encouraged Vincent to walk home without me. He is still in training, but definitely old enough to walk back up the hill with a friend. He began to shrug me off a few months ago: where he used to happily hold my hand as we walked into school, I noticed that he began to let go in advance. I wasn't hurt. I have looked after too many children to take their milestones personally. I just thought okay, that's where we are. Yet I am always hesitant before he knocks at the front door, just in case he needs me. Lily and Jackson are seasoned independents who thrive with more freedom and responsibility.

Abby has an air of premature independence about her, I notice. She seems somehow very much 'inside' herself – it's the only way I can describe it. I watch her for a little longer through the window as she rushes round the garden saving herself.

They all like a snack when they get in. A bag of crisps will do for now while they meet their new friend Abby. I have them out ready, but they don't come to the front door. They must have all congregated together on the front door step and decided to collectively come round the back. Maybe they are a little nervous. Some of our anxiety prior to Abby's arrival may well have rubbed off, however much we tried to keep it hidden. They open the back gate and see the little brown-haired girl bombing round the garden as though her life depended on it.

They stand there and gawp at her. I wave from the window; they all smile, caught in the act.

Abby suddenly sees them and runs over. 'You want to play?' she calls, with a surprising degree of self-assurance. All three smile and slip into their older, more sophisticated selves – which I know won't last long. Abby chats away, telling them about the garden. Lily engages the most: she nods and walks around with Abby, pretending to be surprised by all that she has discovered. The boys come into the kitchen and say hello.

Jackson asks, with his classic frankness, 'How long is she staying?'

That's my boy – I have learnt that this is his 'teenage self', always a tad on the grumpy side. I smile and offer a bag of crisps to avoid answering the question. Vincent has noticed that Abby is on his scooter. Of course he has, nothing gets past him. I ask if it's okay and apologise profusely and explain that the scooter she came with was too tall and broken, probably dangerous.

Vincent, who is always kind and gets a kick out of being useful or doing a good deed says, 'Yes, sure. That's okay. I hope she enjoys it.'

If he's honest with himself, he also knows that he hasn't used it for a year and he got a stunning new bike for Christmas that has made the scooter redundant. I can rationalise this, so I'm hoping – and assuming – that he has maturely evaluated the situation.

I carry on watching from the window and see Abby reach out to hold hands with Lily, who politely obliges. That's good to see. When Lily came to our home she too had been through an awful lot and would not hold my hand for four years. She hated physical contact, believing it to be somehow wrong. Every child I have met who has experienced trauma has a different response to physical contact. You cannot easily quantify attachment disorder; each affected child may offer a different response. Lily brings Abby into the kitchen. I suspect she just wants to drop her off while she gets changed out of her uniform and sorts out her school bag.

With the complicated Nigerian rice dish I was planning to cook no longer a welcoming requirement, and a quick wave of gratitude that I didn't manage to find those yams, I ask Abby if she likes pasta.

'YES, PASTA!' she shouts, too loudly for the small space.

'That's good,' I say, deliberately modelling the calmest of 'indoor voices'. Most children eat pasta in some form or another. 'I thought I would make a cheesy pasta bake for us all tonight.' Straightforward taste and good comfort food for all: usually a winner. I make a salad to go alongside. This is particularly for Jackson, who has now started attending the gym as well as joining the local town rugby team and has become the most health-conscious member of the family. I am thrilled, as a few months ago he might have been considered to be a little overweight and could not be left unaccompanied with the Nutella jar. I am convinced that if the adults eat well and healthily then the children will follow eventually, even if that is a long time coming. I mix in the sauce, grate some more cheese for the top and put the pasta in the oven to bake. Suddenly Abby is standing next to me holding the little cuddly rabbit.

'I love her!' she says. I don't think she realises that I have given it to her – even more magical for her than a gift is the idea the rabbit simply appeared, just for her.

I am so pleased she likes the rabbit. I would have been worried that her first night in a strange house in a new family, without any kind of comfort or soother, would be so very hard. She stands and hugs the rabbit as though it is her dearest possession, which I suppose that now it might indeed be, and strokes its face tenderly. Then, suddenly, Abby drops it on the floor and walks off. All interest in the rabbit is gone. Strange.

I quickly rescue the toy before Doug does something antisocial. It wouldn't be the first time: he has a history of demonstrating affection towards a foster child's soft toy. Last time it was in front of the social worker; that was fairly embarrassing. Social workers have the power to demand that your dog is put down if they think your dog is a risk to a foster child. I don't know whether Douglas being a sex pest to a child's soft toy constitutes a threat, but nothing would surprise me. Lily and Vincent are watching TV in the sitting room. I assume Abby is in there with them as I begin to lay the table.

I call the children to the table.

Abby comes flying into the kitchen, but from an unexpected direction: straight out of my studio. Now I'm worried. I have two portraits set up on easels that are nearing completion. I am filled with a dread that shoots from my core and wants to scream. I stop myself from running in there straight away, in spite of my horrible foreboding.

Instead, I ask the children to wash their hands. They all lie and say that they have. I let it pass. We have eight chairs set around the kitchen table, each a different colour. The children all have their favourite colours and places. Jackson's is an orange carved wooden chair; Lily prefers an old kitchen chair done in turquoise with a circular back; and Vincent's choice is an old-fashioned school chair painted a soft green. There are several colours still available: red, yellow, blue, stripped wood and pink. I place Abby in the red chair. I never like to make the girl-pink connection, and anyway I have seen enough of her behaviour this afternoon to suggest that she is not really a pink kind of girl.

But neither is she red.

'No.'

She swaps it for a little dark wooden chair – that is tiny and no one really uses. Okay, fair enough, I made the wrong choice. I grab a pile of cushions from an armchair in the corner and pop them under Abby so that she can reach the table. I take the pasta bake out of the oven and place it on the mats in the centre of the table. There are a number of serving spoons. I ask Abby how much she would like.

She watches the other children pile up their plates for a moment.

'Like that.'

I put a neat pile on her plate – that she hoovers in seconds. I ask if she would like more. She has four portions.

Jackson who holds the Allen world record for food consumption, looks on in amazement. 'Steady on there, Abby!'

Abby just laughs. She has food all round her plate, down her front and around her face. Lily looks on in disgust as Abby continues to eat loudly with her mouth wide open, talking and spitting out food at the same time. It is quite the sight to behold. She switches between using a fork and her fingers.

I wonder why her adoptive family never tackled this. And the other foster carers, for that matter. She has been in the care system for nearly a year, too; how has nobody tried to help her learn how to eat properly? This is really distressing, and unacceptable – unpleasant for everyone else around the table. Why is she eating so badly?

I notice, too, how she struggles to keep still. She is wriggling about on her chair, even while in the act of eating.

Lily has had enough when Abby begins waving her fork around and pointing at things around the kitchen. 'No, not like that at the table,' she warns. 'Keep your arms to yourself.'

More food is spat across the table.

'Can you keep your mouth closed, just while you are eating?' Lily pleads. I can see that she is really struggling, and it is obscene. My work is cut out for me as far as mealtimes are concerned, I can already tell.

At that moment Lloyd wanders in to make a coffee to take back to his studio. He quickly sizes up the situation, moves behind Abby and whispers to her, 'Sit up nicely at the table, there's a good girl.'

'Fuck off,' says Abby in response.

Lloyd takes a step backwards, away from the table.

The children all look at each other and then me. I widen my eyes and shake my head.

'Abby, please don't use that word. It's a horrible word and we don't use it here.'

She looks at me with what seems to be genuine confusion. 'Why not?'

I change tack. 'Abby, have you heard people use that word before?'

She looks directly at me and, spitting out more pasta across the table, says, 'Mum and Dad said it – and that other one.'

I don't know who 'that other one' is, but I don't press her. I hope it wasn't another foster carer.

'Well, I'm sorry to hear that, Abby – but that's not a good word, it's not one we want to hear in this house. Please don't use it again.'

She laughs, spluttering more food around her.

Jackson finishes his meal quickly, asking if he might leave the table. His request is swiftly followed by one from Vincent and one from Lily. There are unfamiliar mutterings about urgent needs to tackle homework. Normally I have to nag them to do their homework but tonight that seems more appealing than being at this dining table with Abby, clearly.

Does she know that she has caused this reaction? She sits laughing like a mad old woman, wriggling around in her seat, those carefully piled cushions now scattered across the floor. At least the dogs are happy: they are busy cleaning up the spilt and spat-out food from the tiles.

I look at Lloyd, who lingers in the doorway, a grimace clouding his face before he walks away. I ask Abby to wipe her hands before she goes to play. I notice that while she waits for me to rinse the dish cloth her arms flap continuously against her sides. She holds out her hands and shakes them, manically; so much that I can hear her wrists clicking. It is a noise that will become horribly familiar. I manage, somehow, to wipe her hands and most of the food from her face.

'Would you like a nice bath?' I ask, mindful that this will be a good way to get the rest of the food off as much as a relaxing opportunity for Abby before bedtime.

She jumps up and down with excitement. I leave the kitchen, abandoning the delighted dogs to their unofficial dinner, and go upstairs with Abby, who is now holding my hand. What were those words on her referral form? *A very loving child, who thrives on the attention of adults.*

We reach the bathroom and prepare the bath to be filled: putting the slip mat in place and choosing some bubbles. I put the bubble bath on the side and get a clean towel out of the drawer. I walk with Abby to her bedroom and let her choose pyjamas, conscious that I can now detect an unmistakable wee smell.

I hope that she doesn't notice the sniff. 'Do you need to go to the toilet before you get in?'

In answer she pulls down her trousers and pees straight onto the bedroom floor, too fast for me to stop it. Abby laughs and runs along the hall to the bathroom. The next sound I hear is a big splash. I grab another towel and throw it on the wee. Like the disaster area that is now my kitchen, I will just have to come back to this later. I head quickly to the bathroom to find a very naked girl jumping off the side of the bath into the water, displacing much of it as she does so.

She is laughing and has the bubble bath bottle in her hands, squirting it all over the bath as though she is firing a gun. Within a few seconds, before I am able to react, all the bubble bath is in the water, now foaming up nicely.

I ask Abby to get into the bath and sit down or she will hurt herself.

'Fuck off,' is the verbal response, but she also begins running on the spot in the bath, an action that ensures that water and bubbles go everywhere.

Asking nicely has achieved nothing. I put my hand into the bath to pull on the plug and let out some of the water. She bends down and bites my arm as I am reaching through the foam.

I yelp.

Jackson comes running at the sound, perhaps also alerted by the commotion that has been building before. He takes in the scene and does a double-take.

'Whoa there! Are you alright, mum?'

'Yes, thanks, luvvy, all good,' I lie, nursing my arm. 'I think Abby is just a little excited.'

As if to prove the point, she now lies down on her front, splashing her arms around as though she is swimming, whilst singing 'swim away, swim away' at the top of her voice.

I look at Jackson whose face says exactly what I'm thinking: what the hell have we got here? The answer is that I have no idea. Normally I would leave the door ajar and busy myself around the bedrooms leaving a child to play nicely in the bath, but I daren't move. I don't think it would be safe to leave Abby for a minute, a second.

There is water all over the floor, but I can't lean in and touch the plug or she might bite me again. We remain like this for nearly 40 minutes, Abby regularly 'changing the game' to cause increasing levels of chaos and ever more foam and bubbles to be flung around the bathroom. As well as running on the spot, pretend-swimming and jumping off the sides, she smacks the sponge against the tiles and tries to catch it as though it is a ball. All the time she keeps up a tuneless singing that is occasionally offset by random shrieking. I am soaked, the fluffy bath mat is a saturated mess, there are puddles of water all over the floor and disintegrating bubbles slide down every surface.

Eventually, the remaining bathwater begins to cool; surely the novelty must be wearing off by now?

'Time to get warm and dry, Abby?' I gently coax, holding out a towel.

It isn't time to get warm and dry, apparently.

Another 20 minutes pass before she can be persuaded to come out.

But after all the procrastination, now the actual getting out happens all of a sudden. Before I have a chance to get hold of her arm to help, she has flung herself out of the bath, crashed into the towel rail, landed with a sickening thump, and is now laying naked on the floor, laughing and swishing around on the wet boards.

Lloyd stands at the door. 'What's going on?'

He looks at my face and asks again, 'Louise, what's happening here?'

I can offer nothing more than a helpless shrug.

'Abby, you need to get up and dressed.'

Abby laughs and says, 'Fuck off, fatty.'

Just as downstairs, Lloyd backs away, knowing better than to tackle this now, but we share a knowing look.

Eventually Abby puts on her pyjamas. It takes an age, and my usually ready supply of patience is severely deplet-ed, so I decide against the usual routine with children after a bath – which might ordinarily involve a bit of TV or a story downstairs. Instead I get Abby into her room and straight into bed.

I have a selection of books she can choose from. Abby chooses a book more suited to a younger child, with no real narrative and only a few words on each page. I pull the chair from the wall over towards the bed; all my instincts say, 'Do not sit on the bed with this child in it.' She sits up and giggles. She does a lot of that. I also notice her hand shaking again and hear the clicks of her wrists.

'Does that hurt?' I ask.

More laughter. 'NO!'

I read the same book five times. Each time we reach the end she says, 'Again!' like a baby or toddler might. When I say 'no' to a sixth reading, she asks if she can sit in bed and read it by herself.

'Yes, but only for half an hour. Then I will come and tell you to go to sleep.'

She nods and giggles again.

I pick the towel off the floor and soak up as much as I can of the damp patch from earlier.

'Do you know where the toilet is?'

She nods and performs the little giggle again. I am starting to find the sound really unsettling.

'Are you sure? Tell me,' I say, not convinced.

She gives me the exact location of three toilets, including very precise 'landmarks' around the house. She must have noted them all when she was with Lloyd. This is a big and confusing house, so it's an impressive feat in a short space of time. Clearly she has a good internal sat nav.

I get the anti-bacterial spray and a cloth and am bent over scrubbing at the wee when she hits me, hard, across the head.

It takes me completely by surprise, and hurts.

'No, Abby. That is wrong. You must not hurt anyone.'

She laughs and pretends to read the book. I know that she is pretending and not actually reading because she is pointing at pictures of animals and saying the names out loud: cat, dog, horse, duck, and so on.

Then another narrative develops involving the animals and an adventure. She has returned to the theme of rescuing Abby. In spite of my frustrations over the whole bath-time episode, I take stock of this once more and wonder exactly what is going on for this child. I repeat that I will be back in half an hour to say goodnight. She doesn't look up from the book and the made-up story.

I mop up the bathroom and clean out the bath. I head down to the kitchen and clear up the table. I am exhausted, but also dreadfully concerned. The half hour is up. I go back upstairs to say good night to Abby. I walk into her room, so carefully prepared, that now looks like a war zone. She has ripped up every page into tiny, tiny pieces and surrounded herself with them. Laughing, she sits in the middle of the devastation without a care in the world. There is no sense of remorse – nothing, in fact, behind her eyes at all. The eyes might be the windows to the soul, but right now hers seem like the doors to an empty room.

I pick up as much as I can and put the fragments of paper into the bin. I am a little sad – that was one of Vincent's old reading books – but foster carers have little room for sentimentality.

I ask her if she would like the door open and the light on or off.

'Shut the door, please; and keep the light on.'

I am at least pleased by the 'please' squeezed in there. I do as she asks but hang around for a bit to see if she is settling down.

When she seems quiet I finally go to my studio. I work from home as an artist and this is my sanctuary as well as my workplace. I think I know what I am going to find, but still look in horror at the mess on the table and floor. My sketchbooks have been pulled all over the floor from the pile on the chest. She has opened tube after tube of acrylic paint and squeezed the colour onto the floor. Worse, blue paint has been smudged all across the face of my commissioned portrait: two weeks' worth of work. Opposite my studio is a sink room. That is also blue: she must have calmly walked over and washed her hands, once her handiwork was complete. A little water clears her of this deed.

I feel sick. All that work. This is my livelihood. I try to fight back the anger, and lose. I bend down and begin to clear up the chaos through gritted teeth and mental cursing.

Lloyd appears. 'Oh my God,' he says, taking in the destruction.

I sink right down to the floor.

'What have we done?'

Chapter 4

Having no social workers to call upon directly, and having no responses to my calls and emails from any of the managers, leaves me feeling quite desolate. I know that to be in this situation is illegal, without even beginning to consider the moral dimension, and it worries me greatly. Where will we be if something happens to Abby – or to us? Her behaviour so far has confirmed all my worst fears. She is a danger to herself, and a physical threat to the rest of us, in spite of being so young, and undersized.

I find Kate's number amongst the paperwork as she promised, and leave several messages for her.

I am beginning to feel that we have been set up.

They needed Abby out of the area so they didn't have to deal with her and her complex needs. All my gut feelings were right. This child is full of issues. I feel angry and let down. We have looked after children with FAS before, and we had to call notice on each placement because we didn't get the support we needed to help the child. We have been through some dark times looking after these children because it is specialist work and we are just mainstream foster care workers; but, as we all know, the 'out-there' cases are the new mainstream. What is mainstream? Mainstream does not really exist anymore, thanks to drink and drugs and mobile phones. We are dealing with incredibly complicated children in family homes with the smallest and most inadequate of tool kits.

I send more emails, much stronger than the first. I carbon copy them to every social worker I have spoken to: Annie, Kate, their managers, the head of children's social care. I stop short of copying in the Prime Minister, but only just.

I know that I will never hear from them directly. They will simply send it to a manager who will eventually send it to whichever social worker ends up on our watch, but it gives me the temporary illusion of 'acting'. I feel as though I am drowning in my concerns about Abby.

Lloyd is not impressed at all. 'We have to move her on, Louise; we have been here before.'

That isn't helping me either, because I know that he is right, but I don't want to be part of the problem in a strained system. I feel stressed. My mind wanders. We looked after a little boy, Bobby – a year or so ago – who was a similar age to Abby. He made allegations against Lloyd. Actually, that's unfair. He didn't make the allegations directly. Bobby actually said something off-hand to his classroom assistant who passed it on to a social worker. It warranted a home visit. I was in our bedroom folding laundry on the big trunk in the bay window as they passed by towards the front door.

I knew the odds were stacked against us when I overheard her say to her manager, 'See, I told you she lived in a big house.' It was the adults who made the complaint. Five-year-old Bobbie forgot what he said and couldn't think of a reason that Lloyd had upset him in any way.

It later transpired that he had made exactly the same comment about every man he had met, but it felt to me as though the adults around us had been determined to undermine our reputation. It has made both Lloyd and me wary. Like him, I can only see trouble ahead. But we also know that we are talking about a little girl who was rejected at birth and has lived in five different homes with five different families in six years. She needs a chance. And if we give the '28-day notice' to return her from our care, there will be a fallout. We have to think carefully about this.

Once the other children have gone to bed, I sit with Lloyd in the kitchen. We have a glass of wine each, and it is only Monday.

The first thing that I do is forgive Abby everything she did today. It isn't easy. I am really, really upset about my artwork, and the invasion of a private space in my home – the sanctity of my studio has been violated. My other children have been distressed by Abby's actions at the dining table. I have been physically hit and bitten. I have spent a great deal of time cleaning up after her, and an old book – with a nostalgic value to it – has been destroyed. The only way I can attain a state where I can forgive is to try to imagine what it is like to *be* her.

I am in very little doubt that Abby has FAS, and Lloyd agrees. I begin to research as much as I can about it – knowing already that there is no cure, just plans and strategies.

I also order some books online that deal more theoretically with attachment. I will become a scholar in these areas. I need to understand the legal and emotional support we can advocate for her. I can pull on so much from my own childhood – in relation to her inability to make sense of the relationships around her, definitely. I know what it feels like not to know who to trust, and perhaps more importantly, who not to. Google tells me that this is 'Disinhibited Social Engagement Disorder (DSED)'. It is about not feeling any fear or hesitancy when meeting someone for the first time – being over-familiar, or over-friendly. It doesn't sound too bad on one level, though it's a serious clinical condition that needs treatment. But I *get* it. FAS, though, I don't. The damage is physical – to the brain, as well as to other internal organs – and it feels scary. It's a huge amount for a little person to bear. And, I remind myself, it's not her fault.

I manage to convince Lloyd that we need to be strategic and get all the medical and educational work done – and soon. In the absence of any professional support, I decide to create my own plan.

First on the list is to take Abby to my GP to begin the paediatric assessment process. I will phone first thing in the morning to get that going. Satisfied that we have a way to move forward, we turn off the lights, put the dogs to bed and head to bed ourselves. I think I have forgiven everything she did today as we climb the stairs.

But as we reach the landing I can hear something heavy – furniture, perhaps, being dragged in Abby's room. What now?

I open her bedroom door to find this tiny girl redesigning her room. She has, somehow, moved *everything*. The bed is now along the far wall. It has been dragged almost the length of the room. The wardrobe is in a different place. The IKEA drawers are in the opposite corner to where they began. Everything that was on the shelves has been taken down and is now arranged on the little table, that has been positioned near the bed. Where has she got her energy, not to mention her *strength*, from?

She turns to face us in the doorway, where we are standing open-mouthed.

'This is much better, isn't it? Do you like it?'

I look at Lloyd, who blows out his cheeks and walks to the bathroom.

'It's nice to have everything the way you want it, but now that you have, it's really time for sleep. Young girls need their sleep to grow.'

I usher her back to bed. It occurs to me that she hasn't said either of our names at any point.

'Abby? Do you remember what our names are?' I ask as I pull the duvet cover back across her.

She looks at me and does that little giggle, 'No.'

I remind her that I am Louise and say Lloyd's name, making her repeat both of them back to me.

'Goodnight, Abby. Sleep!' I repeat.

But sleep is not yet on the agenda for Abby, and therefore not for us. We lie in bed listening to another hour's worth of movement before it finally goes quiet. I get out of bed and look in on her. No matter that she has moved the bed and changed the room around, she is lying in the middle of the floor on top of the duvet, with two pillows resting on her. I fetch some additional blankets and cover her. I do not want to risk waking her. I lie back down in bed myself, but sleep is elusive now: my mind is spinning with the day's events, and with what we are going to do next. I don't know what tomorrow will bring. I can only stick to the plan we have made.

Abby is awake before dawn. At 5am I can hear sounds of movement about the house. It takes me a moment to process the sound. I step out of the bedroom.

She has found my laundry cupboard and pulled most of it out. My pristine laundry cupboard, whose order gives me peace of mind. My eyes are stinging and my mouth is dry, but I will myself not to be cross.

Wearily I say, 'Abby, you should be in bed.'

'No. I'm awake.'

Right then. I reach out my hand towards her. 'Breakfast, then?'

She seems keen on this idea so we walk down to the kitchen. I open up the cupboard and ask her to choose some cereal. Before my brain has had time to kick in, she has made her choice: chocolate squares; the children's weekend breakfast. Wrong on a couple of levels, but I gave her the choice. I get a bowl and sit down with Abby at the kitchen table. I find a spoon and some milk. I fill the bowl half full and watch her eat the cereal. Unsurprisingly, her eating habits haven't improved overnight.

I ask her gently not to talk while eating and explain why I think that's a good idea. She does so, for half a minute; then forgets and splutters chocolate milk all over herself and the table. I pull off a few sheets of kitchen roll to mop up the mess. I put the coffee machine on and prepare myself for a long day. No, make that a long week. She begins school next week. This girl does not stop. She has made all manner of physical exertion in her bedroom 'Grand Design', has had hardly any sleep at all – and still seems to function at full throttle.

It is at these moments that fostering seems a big ask. It is not helpful to do the financial calculations: we earn around 30 pence an hour to do this. I have to dig pretty deep sometimes and stop myself from throwing in the towel. Right now feels like one of those moments. With no sleep myself, this is all feeling a bit too difficult.

I know, too, that I need to protect the other children. They have seen some alarming behaviour from fostered children over the years. Even Lily, whom we love dearly as one of our own, had some incredibly interesting behaviour when she arrived – that lasted for the best part of a year before it began to subside.

Once I get the ball rolling with Abby's health and education assessments, we will have a better idea where we are – and I will certainly be asking why this hasn't happened before.

And we can't throw in the towel. If we did stop fostering, we would probably lose Lily. Her birth family would never let us adopt her, and the other alternative – Special Guardianship – does not have great press amongst the fostering community. You have all the work and responsibility and less support. And that is a problem because you can never know what's around the corner, what demons are going to surface for a traumatised child, what support will be needed.

So: I am going to stay strong for Abby.

I am.

Chapter 5

Upstairs, I walk past the mess from my beautiful airing cupboard. I step over my soaps, stored in there to make everything smell nice. I wonder if I can get away with refolding the sheets and pillow cases, or whether they will need ironing again. I look at some muddy marks and footprints that have found their way onto the linen and decide that it's all going to need washing.

But I don't have time for that right now because I managed to get an appointment at the GP surgery for Abby.

I have sent emails to Annie and Kate – and someone this end – to let them know I am doing this. A paper trail is vital: a foster carer can never take for granted that everyone knows what's going on. Sometimes it feels like the whole system is run on a wing and a prayer. If anything goes wrong then the finger is always pointed at the foster carer first. That's why I write my logs, and carbon copy people in to emails – managers where possible, and their line managers too, if I can. I know this seems too much, and I know that some people don't like it: the chain of command in children's social care is rigid and people get offended if you go above them – but when a child needs help and I need to get something done, then, frankly, I pay no attention to the hierarchy and do what I can for the child. I am here to advocate for them.

There is usually a fallout. Sometimes disgruntled social workers have tried finding issues to make complaints about me or Lloyd – which is what I think happened in Bobbie's case last year – and is the reason why I keep good, detailed, accurate records.

With permission of participants, I have regularly used my phone to record a meeting ensuring that I include the date and time at the start, a bit like a police interview. Perhaps I have seen one too many crime dramas on a Sunday evening, but it works for me. It's sad that as a foster carer you have to use these measures, but I have found that social workers are more mindful about what they say when they are being recorded, and that can only be a good thing.

If they refuse to be recorded then I might invite a fellow foster carer to take accurate notes that we read back at the end of the meeting. Since austerity measures have kicked in, standards of practice have dropped. And, following a couple of high-profile cases in the media where social services were criticised (who hasn't heard of Baby 'P'?) the rapid implementation of policy changes has sometimes been carried out with more concern for box-ticking than people-fixing. All manner of poor practice has seeped into this sector. It sometimes feels as though one might have more sense of security in a lawless Wild West. Consequently, over the last few years foster carers have fought back and are demanding their rights and protection – me included.

The trouble is that there is no shared place of work – no staff canteen to meet and chat – and that can make you feel vulnerable and alone. Foster carers work in isolation. That means that effectively we are divided, and often conquered – but we care so much for the children who come into our care that we fight for them to have what they are entitled to.

The spending cuts have made this sector a pretty hard terrain. Managers tell social workers not to spend money, but our children *need* the money. It is rightfully theirs, or should be, through our taxation system. How else can they repair and aim to have a good and useful life? When I have advocated before for children with FAS who we have looked after, I have found closed doors, delayed meetings and all manner of stalling tactics.

The worst comment I think I have heard came from one manager after I described the behaviour of a 12-year old girl with FAS who had been sexually exploited in her area by a known paedophile. I pleaded for this child is be given proper therapeutic support.

'She can't receive therapy until she settles,' the manager told me.

I said, 'And she will *never* settle as long as she is reliving her trauma every day.'

My 'assertiveness' that day earned a complaint. But it demonstrates the catch-22 situation that we find ourselves in so regularly. That's why I keep good records, and that's why foster carers have to have nerves of steel.

So, because I have still not been given a supervising social worker, nor has Abby been given her social worker, I intend to use this opportunity to get as much in place as possible for her before any further funding cuts or delays are put in place.

I sit Abby on a booster seat in the back of the car. On goes Kiss FM. All the children (and me too, if I'm honest) prefer that station and get very annoyed when Lloyd has the cheek to leave another radio station on – in his car. We head off to the doctors and then I think we might go into town to buy some new clothes and bits and bobs to keep Abby going.

In the surgery waiting room I notice how fidgety Abby is. She can't keep still at all. Her legs kick incessantly at her chair; she shakes her hands so much that her wrists click again. Perhaps I am being unduly bothered by that. It makes me feel funny – a bit like when people pull their fingers and make them click. I just don't like it. When she catches my eye I smile as though I'm not bothered by the sound or the action. She looks at me quite a lot, but it is in quick, shifty glances – she can't stay focused.

When she gets very lively I gently touch her arm and 'shh' her.

'Try to sit as still as you can,' I suggest.

She nods obligingly, which is an improvement on 'fuck off', but then is off again straight away.

In the corner of the doctors' waiting room is a wooden activity centre for babies and toddlers. When my sons were little I dreaded them playing with it, touching the different components alongside all the other sniffing children. I have always perceived it as a germ station – but it interests Abby. She gets up from her chair – which means that the kicking stops – for which I am grateful. She sits up on her knees playing with little beads, pushing them along a wire. She pushes some a little too hard, but has little sense of what's appropriate for a communal toy in a surgery waiting room. Fellow patients look on with faces that seem to say, 'Keep your child under control.'

I wish I could hold up a sign saying 'Foster carer – doing my best for 30p an hour – give us a break'.

There is a bit of a wait. My mind wanders around the waiting room and all its tattered posters. I remember looking after a 13-year-old girl who, when she came to the supermarket with me, pestered me to buy her a bottle of vodka. It was all she wanted.

I said no what felt like a thousand times in different ways, but she kept going. She was begging me very loudly as we walked through the aisles.

I refused again, and again, and again.

But she couldn't take that 'no' as a final answer, and climbed into a large freezer that had 20 varieties of chips stacked in it. She stood atop them, and, at the top of her lungs, cried out to her shopper audience, 'She's evil, she is. She won't buy me vodka.'

Part of me thought that this was outrageously funny – and in many ways I suppose it was – but the other bit of me was embarrassed, which is exactly why she did it.

The store manager marched up to me with his clipboard, stern face and a hissed, 'Will you keep your child under control?'

'I would love to,' I responded. 'She is a traumatised foster child who arrived three days ago. If you have any suggestions then I'm all ears.'

At which point he backed off. And I began to walk out. She, like most children, suddenly wanted to be with their adult rather than being left alone. No vodka was purchased. So although we're not quite at those levels, here in the waiting room, I can sense the same judgement from the other waiting patients.

Abby is in her own little world. She seems relatively happy, if ever so slightly aggressive with the beads, but who am I to judge bead movement for a small child who has lived with five families in her short years? I am touched that every so often she looks up and gives me a little wave. I smile and wave back. I am definitely 'her adult' in this environment.

Eventually her name comes up and off we go.

I ask her to press the big blue button to open the door. She gives it an almighty punch and I feel the looks from the waiting room. Thankfully it works without requiring further maintenance and we continue up to the doctor's door, on which I give a little knock.

'Come in.'

We enter together and I ask Abby to sit down. I sit next to her on another nearby chair. The doctor is in his mid-thirties, deck shoes: so many doctors seem to go sailing that I wonder if it is part of the entrance exam. The doctor looks up from his computer and asks Abby a few questions.

Or at least he tries.

Within a few seconds Abby has slid down from the chair and is up running around the doctor's office, pulling things off the shelves, jumping on the black examination bed, ripping the white paper from the roll.

I choose not to intervene. I sit and look at the doctor, who also lets her carry on for a few minutes. The doctor asks me how long she has been with me.

'Since yesterday afternoon,' I reply, much more brightly than I feel.

I explain how it feels rather as though she has been dumped from another county the other side of the country.

The doctor raises his eyebrows. 'If that's the case, then they saw you coming.'

I do feel like a bit of a chump, to hear him say it so caustically as that. 'You really think I've been played? I didn't think they would do a thing like that.'

He laughs. 'Oh, I think you and I both know that they would.'

He types 'Abimbola' in to his computer, frowning and doing a slight double-take as he does so. While he waits for her file to appear, I look over at Abby, who is now tearing the white paper up into little tiny pieces. The doctor follows my glance. We share a tight, helpless smile.

I tell the doctor that although I have not been given any paperwork regarding education and health, I have my suspicions that Abby has Foetal Alcohol Syndrome.

'Well, yes, I think we can safely say that's a given. And I am fairly certain we could add a few more labels to that: the main one being neglect.'

I feel my heart sink a little.

'I would also say Attention Deficit Hyperactivity Disorder – ADHD,' he continues. 'But she would have to be tested for that by the paediatrician.' He peers at the screen. 'Actually, it looks like testing for FAS *was* started a couple of years ago by… yes, I assume that must be her adoptive mother, but it wasn't completed and hasn't been followed up.'

'Well, that's strange. The social worker said that there was no record, and that she didn't think she had FAS.'

He looks directly at me. 'It's all over her file. There's no way they can't have known.'

Now I feel really angry – and hurt. We *have* been totally hoodwinked. There is no question. Worse, they may have actually lied to us in order to get us to take Abby. I can just imagine Lloyd's response to this piece of news.

'Ok, so can we can get the assessment process started all over again?'

'Oh, definitely.'

He taps away at the keyboard for a moment, and then turns to Abby, who has now created a reasonably sized mountain of torn paper and has begun finding other inventive ways of playing with the roll, one of which includes turning it into a superhero cape and jumping from the window ledge. I am thankful that we are on the ground floor, and that the doctor remains mild-mannered.

'Can I have a look at you, Abby? See my torch, here? I'm just going to shine this little torch into your eyes. It might make you blink for a moment but it's nothing to worry about.'

Abby is perfectly obliging.

'Hmmm. I will also get her booked into the hospital to have her eyes looked at.' He pauses for a moment. 'I'm not an expert but I would say she might have a lazy eye.'

Ears are next. Abby is fascinated by the whole process and sits as still as I have seen her in the whole time since she arrived.

'I think she might need her ears drained. Does she seem to have problems hearing?'

Up until this moment I have assumed that Abby's hearing is selective. Now, given what the doctor has just said, I'm not so sure. I am honest with the doctor.

There is a plea in my voice and in my eyes as I say, 'Is there anything – anything at all – I can give her to slow her down or help her sleep?'

The doctor frowns again.

I try harder. 'I need help. She was like this until one o'clock this morning, and then up again at five. I have to work in the day and I have three other children.'

'I think you need to have a frank conversation with her social worker.'

I laugh, just because I don't know how else to react. 'She hasn't been assigned one here yet, and the old one is miles away on the other side of the country – and doesn't answer her phone.'

The doctor sits back in his chair and lets out a whistle. 'You are going to have to fight, you know. Or they will leave her with you.' He winks. 'You didn't hear that from me.'

I feel better for his support, but worse for realising what is happening to us, and just how rubbish it is.

'The only thing I can suggest is that you give her the recommended dose of children's antihistamine before bedtime. It's not ideal, but it might just take the edge off.' Gently, he adds, 'I know this is not what you are going to want to hear, and I will do what I can to speed things up, but the referral and assessment process can take up to five months.'

I want to cry. I fall short of asking if there is something that *I* can take to help me get through this.

As we make our way into town, I think about what the doctor has told me about the fact that an initial referral was started by Abby's adoptive mother. That tells me that she must have cared about her. But why wasn't it followed up? Why did nothing else happen? Then I think about the other placements that have broken down since she left the adopted family. Given that it is the foster carers' job to sort out all medical appointments, I'm not surprised they broke down without an understanding of Abby's condition. Her behaviour, without a diagnosis, simply looks naughty and destructive. Out of control, at times. But if her brain has been physically damaged by the alcohol then it is going to function differently from that of other children. She will see the world differently, experience everything on a different level. Factor in the rejection, and the doctor's suggestion of neglect, and you have a recipe for carnage. No wonder she is off the wall. I want to help, but the reality is that I don't know that we can do this for very long. It has been less than 24 hours and I am utterly exhausted.

We go to a department store that sells clothes and homeware. We browse the children's clothes. I pick out one or two things that I think might suit Abby, but she is not interested in any of the dresses or leggings that I select. I hold out a princess dressing-up outfit in bright pink with a silver wand and crown. Irresistible to some children. She is entirely nonplussed. Instead she runs up to the boys' fancy dress section and picks out a dark costume that looks like something the grim reaper might wear. It has a sort of helmet-mask attached and it takes me a moment to realise it's a Darth Vader costume. I'm not a particular fan of Star Wars, but she seems to love it. She holds it up against herself.

'Can I have this, Wendy? Please?'

'Not if you call me "Wendy", I say. 'My name's Louise.'

'Sorry,' she says, with the characteristic little laugh.

'I really like it. Can I have it?'

It seems like an odd choice, but what do I know? 'Yes, you can have it. But we need to find you some other clothes as well.'

She holds the grim black costume under one arm, stroking the shiny black plastic of the helmet part, and looks very happy. It bears some resemblance to the mask that she picked up yesterday and was so fascinated by. Perhaps that is what has drawn her to it. I collect a few sweatshirts and a school polo shirt and skirt. We pick up some new underwear and a light raincoat. She came without any kind of coat, but it isn't that cold anymore, so a raincoat will be enough for the time being. We sit down to try on some school shoes. She refuses point blank to try on any of the buckled girls' shoes, and instead selects a clumpy pair of lace-ups from the boys' section. I find it interesting, and wonder how she will fit in with the other girls at school, but I don't want to object to her choice.

As we walk to the till with a new uniform, play clothes and Darth Vader outfit, she notices a blanket in the homeware section in a camouflage design. She buries her face into the fluffy blanket.

'Oooh, this is beautiful.'

Seems a strange choice of adjective, but I pop the blanket in the basket, too. If it makes her happy, who am I to argue?

Chapter 6

When the others arrive home from school, it is to discover Abby covered from head to toe in her Darth Vader robe and mask, bombing round the garden on the scooter. Jackson, alpha male rugby player already a head taller than me at the tender age of 14, looks out of the window.

'Jeees, she's got some energy.' He pauses for a moment. 'Feel the force! Strange choice of outfit, though. She's a *Star Wars* fan, then?'

'I don't think she even has the foggiest idea what *Star Wars* is. Still, that costume seems to have made her very happy.'

Jackson continues to watch her, flying round the lawn as though her life depended on it. 'That's good, isn't it? If it makes her happy. Each to their own, I suppose,' and heads off food hunting in the cupboard.

Lily is more curious and more direct than this.

'But why is she wearing that? Did you *make* her?'

I laugh. 'Not at all! No, she chose it and she loves it.'

And why shouldn't she wear it? I wonder. It probably says more about all of us that we expect to see a slight little girl like Abby in the latest Disney princess dress rather than masked up as a villain. Would I feel happier if it was a little boy dressed up like this? If I'm honest, yes. Part of me wonders where this need to hide in such a sinister outfit comes from. The other part of me thinks, why not? Good on you for skipping past the tiaras.

As we sit down to family dinner number two, I realise quite what hard work mealtimes are going to be. The kindest way that I can describe Abby's table manners is to say that they are somewhat primitive. In fact, she behaves as though she has spent her entire life eating from the floor with no cutlery. I can almost picture her in an animal skin, tearing meat from the bone. But it's strange: it isn't as though she doesn't know what a knife and fork are, just that she prefers not to use them.

Maybe her adoptive mum just wasn't prepared to put the work in to teach her how to sit at a table. And yet that doesn't fit with the tiny amount I know of her: that she was concerned enough to get preliminary medical checks in place for FAS. She cared about Abby, loved her enough to do that – but didn't see it through. I wonder why she gave up on her? I wish Abby had a photo – or something, anything – from her mum. The father sounds like an altogether different beast, disappearing at the first chance. But all I'm doing is piecing together an imaginary life for them from the scantest of references in a file.

We have to have a rethink about bath times, too. Black is clearly a good colour for Abby, though it seems a strange choice for so young a child. I use an eyeliner pencil when we are watching the bath fill up and mark a line in black. She seems to understand that the water must not go any higher. She agrees to this condition, but asks to keep the eyeliner.

This doesn't seem like a terrifically good idea on any level.

'We'll see,' I say, but I think she already knows me well enough to interpret that as a 'no'.

Still, she seems more settled and compliant tonight. I remain hopeful for a better night as she splashes around in the bath much more gently than 24 hours earlier, and plays a game that involves repeatedly diving for treasure. I didn't have much of a chance to look at her body yesterday amidst the competing battles to try and keep her safe and my home in one piece; but tonight, as she has her head submerged but her back in the air, I notice some fairly livid red marks at the left-hand side of her lower back. Instantly they worry me. I remember that William, my adopted brother who was cruelly punished by our adopted mum, bore similar marks. She used to whip William with a belt buckle, and just like William's, Abby's scars are showing up more when they are wet.

'Abby,' I ask, when she has surfaced for air for a moment, 'how did you get those marks on your back?' I point at them and she twists to look.

'Can't tell,' she says, and dives back down to her own Atlantis beneath the bubbles. When she comes back up she sees me still looking so repeats flatly, 'I can't tell you.'

'That's not good, Abby. No one should hit you or hurt you. You know that, don't you?'

'They are there because I am Satan's spawn.'

Her voice turns funny as she says the words, almost as though she has been possessed by some kind of power. Perhaps she is echoing the voice that told her that.

I don't really know quite what to say, only that I want to keep the conversation going, keep the channel of communication open. 'Do you know who Satan is?'

She nods enthusiastically. 'Oh, yes. Satan is bad. Like me.'

It is at this moment that I think I experience my first big surge of empathy for little Abby. Her wide eyes and innocence as she makes this pronouncement pulverise my heart. What could make someone say that? What could make a six-year-old child believe that about themselves? I have no idea what she has been through, but I hope I can gather up enough pieces to begin to build the jigsaw of her life so far.

I sit beside her while she splashes about in the bath, seemingly at peace for now, in spite of her revelation.

I wonder about the best way of getting her to bed tonight and avoiding the stress of the previous evening. This time she climbs out slowly, accepting the guidance of my hand. I help get her dressed. The process seems to be something of a novelty for her. I don't think she quite understands why I am helping her. There is something so resilient and self-sufficient about this girl.

Once in bed I wrap the camouflage blanket around her. She giggles at the softness, shaking her hands to make her wrists click. I hate the sound; it makes me shudder, but I sense that I am just going to have to get used to it. I have left the room more or less as she arranged it last night, just straightening things up a little here and there without interfering with overall design (even though it is not nearly as efficient or aesthetically pleasing as the previous one). Even just edging pieces of furniture an inch or two makes me realise what a feat of strength it must have been for her to move everything around. I am amazed at how such a little person could have lugged such big lumps of furniture across the room. I notice some lovely new scuff marks on the painted floor and remind myself that I can always paint it again. But I am curious about the significance of the room arrangement. I am also curious about Abby's love of black – which seems so incongruous for a six-year-old girl, not to mention the satanic identification. She is a puzzle. A fierce, whirlwind force of a puzzle. I can't help myself. I want to know more. And, after all, it isn't as though she is sleepy.

And I have a plan.

I hold out a drawing book and pencil – irresistible to any child at bedtime as an alternative to sleeping.

'Abby, what was your room like at home with mum and dad? Here's a room…' I quickly sketch out the rough shape of a room. '…where was your door?'

She grabs the pencil and draws something vaguely discernible as a bed against the back wall. She places the wardrobe in the middle of the adjacent wall, along with a chair and a chest of drawers. I look up. It is all looking very familiar.

I ask her to describe what the furniture looked like.

'Brown. Dark brown. Darkest, darkest, darkest brown. And the chair had roses on it.'

It is sad the way that she talks in the past tense, as though the chair itself no longer exists. The way she talks also feels as though the room was very old-fashioned; the sort of furniture you might find in an old person's house – or a rental. Outdated, functional and definitely not a child's room.

'Can you remember the rooms you slept in while you were staying in your other foster homes?'

'No,' she says, very definitely, and shakes her head. I wonder if talking about her old room and home is a good thing or not. Maybe it will stir up lots of memories for her. I draw on my own experiences from growing up in care and think that I would have found it comforting. No matter what went on in that room, it was still the place where I did my dreaming. So I push on.

'Can you remember the carpet?'

She nods. 'It was brown with white patterns. The plug socket was here…' she makes a mark on the drawing. She can remember every little detail and seems to enjoy talking about it. Her tongue pokes out while she concentrates and adds embellishments to the sketch.

I don't need to ask any more questions. A tap has been turned on. She starts a new page, the pencil flying quickly now.

'Charlie is my baby brother. He lived in the room next door.'

'What was that room like?'

She describes a palace more than a nursery. Everywhere is white and shiny. Animal prints and curtain swags, fluffy camouflage blanket (that might explain why we came home with one today), rows of toys and teddies. A silver moneybox, framed photographs, a mobile, a beanbag, a baby armchair, a fluffy rug. It takes much longer to draw Charlie's room. And it feels as though a great deal more effort and money has gone into this room than Abby's – but she doesn't seem to understand that.

No, she wasn't allowed to play in there, 'but I did sneak in in the morning sometimes and make Charlie laugh'. It is a happy memory for her. She laughs as she says it. But it is not the silly giggle that I have found so irritating thus far. Imperceptibly, I have moved closer to her as she tells her story. I stop short of putting my arm around her, though inside I am crying out to. Not only has she lost her mum and dad but this little brother, too. It must be so hard for her to make sense of it all. I hate the unfairness of everything.

After the extensive art session and long conversations about her old house – lo and behold – she finally looks a little tired. The antihistamine from before her bath must be kicking in. She drank it down happily enough. Maybe we will have a better night. Maybe she will settle down and have a lovely long sleep, which I am sure she needs. I hope so; that would make life an awful lot easier. I still have to sort out the other children, fetch in the logs – and the bit I have been putting off: put the bedding back in the airing cupboard. She looks calm and snuggly in her camouflage blanket. I say good night and leave the door open a few inches. The hall light shines through. She seems happy with that.

I do my chores and take a cup of tea back upstairs to have while I carefully fold the sheets and blankets away. It needed a little rearrange, anyhow, I tell myself. As I put the items back into the cupboard I think about Abby's old home – homes – and find that I am curious about how she could not remember anything about the foster placements. She couldn't remember the carers' names; she has only just about learnt mine. I wonder if her brain is only retaining what is important to her, and disregarding everything else. I think her home was very important to her. I am bothered by the stark contrast between the decor in the children's rooms. I would love to know what happened.

I send the other children to bed. Jackson is in his room watching YouTube videos. He loves cooking programmes, so I am happy for him to watch them until 10pm. Lloyd and I watch the news and, as always, I wish I hadn't: terrorist attacks. Now my head is spinning about why our world is so crazy – let alone my own household.

I finish up downstairs while Lloyd heads up before me. But he is back in a few seconds.

'You'd better come and see this,' and he points upstairs.

Abby is back in her Darth Vader costume, manically running up and down the hall, jumping sideways against the walls and generally running amok. She pulls the mask off and her face is covered in thick black streaks – the eyeliner that I forgot to hide.

I take a deep breath.

'Ok, Abby. That's enough, now. Back to bed.'

I send Lloyd off, because if there is one thing I have learnt over the years, it is that a child in full dramatic mode loves an audience. Take the audience away and the child usually becomes bored with the performance.

Not Abby, though.

She runs up and down the hallway and will not stop. When I try to catch her arm she screams out, 'Get off me, bitch!'

Now, I have been here before with foster children, and it's scary. Even the youngest children learn very quickly that they have a superpower: they can 'tell' on you. They can say that you hurt them even if you have not even been anywhere near them. Most foster carers live in dread of this and the guidelines are never clear. Sometimes a child will need restraining for their own safety and that of the adults and other children in the vicinity – but what a policy states and what you think you have learned and understood in any training you have had does not prepare you for the horrible reality of an unfounded allegation.

So, I stand back and let her run it off. Luckily, Vincent and Lily are already asleep, and it takes the decibels of a jet engine to wake them. Jackson is a very knowing, well-informed and tolerant foster sibling, and will have simply decided to keep his head down. He probably has his headphones in anyway.

Time passes. Noisily.

An hour later, Lloyd is sitting up in bed holding a book with his eyes closed.

I am still at one end of the hallway. I watch as Abby finally begins to slow down. I ask her if it's raining. It's not much, but it's my best attempt at distraction technique, being so tired myself.

She scrunches up her forehead. 'No.'

A moment later she pulls the black Darth Vader cloak up over her head. She lays it gently across her chair, climbs into bed and calls out, 'Love you, night night.'

Those little words that should fill my heart with warmth leave me cold.

When a child who barely knows you tells you they love you it saddens me. I have not done anything to deserve their love – certainly not Abby. This is only her second day and much of it has been fraught and fractious. I have never been comfortable with the way some foster carers talk about love. I have never set out to love a foster child: I set out to do right by them.

And I don't feel that I have done terribly well at doing right by Abby.

Chapter 7

Finally I get the call from my new supervising social worker. Her name is Jane and she will be coming over later today to say hello and catch up. When I tell Lloyd he gives it his 'thank cripes for that' face, as though he is a larger-than-life cartoon character.

He follows it with a pointed question. 'Is she going to take her away?'

I shake my head.

Lloyd is looking a little tired, too. It's not surprising. He has a lot of work on at the moment – a contract for a big exhibition in Germany that he is designing the stand and brochures for. I know from past experience that this can be full on and stressful. I am also aware that we have a human dynamo living with us, and this is going to be challenging.

But a new supervising social worker is good news indeed. Though when she knocks on the door, she is a little older than I expected. Her short, bobbed, 'sensible' white hair immediately shouts frumpiness. Oh dear. I invite her in.

She asks me if she should remove her shoes. 'Oh, no need!' I say, gesturing at the floorboards, multiple pairs of shoes belonging to multiple-aged children, and the dogs behind me – but I look down towards her feet. That frumpiness I imagined is immediately belied by her shoes: bright blue, sparkly Dr Martens boots. They seem a little incongruous, like a game of picture consequences with the wrong head put with the wrong feet. I like it. And I'm glad she asked. Kate certainly didn't.

Lloyd has only limited time today and I make her aware of this, though at the same time I myself am aware that this could be misinterpreted. You never know. She might record that *Lloyd was too busy to stay until the end of our meeting*, with all the connotations that might conjure.

She doesn't write anything down, though. Instead she plays with the dogs. I watch Dotty, my faithful human-nature-detector, to see if Jane is on the level. She gets the equivalent of a 'paws up' from Dotty when Dotty jumps straight up onto Jane's lap.

I apologise.

Jane laughs. 'Oh, don't worry. I have three silly dogs of my own. I'm more than used to them. Dotty here can probably smell my three.'

I busy myself making us drinks as I ask, as jovially as I can manage, 'So, have we got a social worker for Abby, yet?'

'No, not as far as I know.'

I roll my eyes; she laughs, and I know straight away that we are going to get on.

'Are you keeping logs?' she asks.

She has no idea how thoroughly kept and right up to date my logs are. I take no risks when it comes to Children's Social Care. I tell Jane all that has happened, which includes a detailed account of Kate's flying visit and keen departure, the lack of records, what happened at the doctors' surgery, what our two night-times so far have been like, and my nascent theories about her adoptive mother.

She sits and looks at us both. Then gives out a long, sighing breath.

'Ok. I'm going to get hold of her – Kate. That's the first thing to do. I'm going to chase her new social worker. And I'm going to call a meeting to create a Care Plan.

I explain that Abby starts school on Monday. 'I'm hoping that going to school will help tire her out.

'I've delivered training on FAS quite recently, and I do truly understand how challenging it can be, I promise you.'

I am feeling as though honesty is the best policy. 'After our other experiences, I have to tell you that I would not have agreed to this referral if we had known that Abby had FAS.'

She goes quiet for a moment as she writes this down.

'We are keen to support and help Abby, but need help ourselves,' I explain.

She looks woeful. It is a face that reads, 'Good luck with that,' and she says, 'Look, I'm not going to beat around the bush. Cuts have ravaged the region. All the social workers have been told that they will have to fund taking a foster child out themselves and that there is no longer a stationery budget. We have to supply all our own diaries and everything.

I smile at this, because I am reminded that when I taught at the university, the powers that be stopped giving out the formerly free yearly academic diary as a money-saving tactic. I share the memory with Jane. 'More staff threatened to walk out over that than over their yearly non-existent pay rise.'

There is more conspiratorial laughter. 'Yes, I suspect there will be a mutiny in my department, too, once news gets out.'

She offers advice about bedtime. 'When she is in bed, come in every few minutes to check her teddy or bring her water or tuck her in so that she knows you're there. If she's getting up repeatedly then she may just be feeling insecure and want to find you.'

Lloyd interjects. 'She hasn't tried to find us. She just ran and ran. Up and down the hall. Incessantly.'

We sit together around the kitchen table, each of us knowing that we have a difficult placement. Worse, none of us have any power or authority to really support Abby's needs in the way that they need to be met. I share my anger that I feel as though she has been 'parked', as far way from her family and previous social workers as possible, and that through no fault of our own they have made Abby somehow 'our problem'.

I know that when I visited the doctor he seemed unsurprised by this crazy theory. Just as then, I work my way through the stages of thinking, 'No, they wouldn't do that!' through, 'They couldn't do that, could they?' to 'They *did* do that.'

Jane can only smile in a conciliatory way, but I do at least begin to feel that it may be a burden shared. At least another person now knows what we are going through, even if she has little power to change it.

We enjoy a companionable silence for a moment. Then I break it by saying, 'Jane, it's time you met Abby. She's in the garden.'

We all get up to walk to the back door. Collectively we see a small girl in a sinister dark robe. Darth Vader is back. Instead of the mask, though, Abby has a bucket on her head. She is spinning round and round, but I can see that the corners of her mouth are curled up into a little smile: she knows that she has an audience.

'Hello Abby,' I call.

She stops spinning and takes off the bucket. She runs up to us and throws her arms around my waist, nestling her head into me.

'I love you, Wendy,' she whispers, but loud enough for everyone to hear, and for Lloyd to frown at the name she has called me.

I lean down and remind her, 'I'm Louise.'

No response.

'Who is Wendy?' I ask, gently.

She looks momentarily puzzled. 'I can't remember.'

I turn back towards Jane with a questioning look. *See. What's that all about?*

Jane steps out into the garden and introduces herself. 'And you must be Abimbola!'

I realise that I haven't filled Jane in fully on that part of the story yet, as Abby responds with the customary giggle and wrist clacking.

'I think "Abby" is—' I pause to find the right word. 'Friendlier.' I make a mental note to discuss that with Jane. We are still no closer to understanding the origins, or significance, of her unusual name.

'Of course. Abby it is. And what have you been up to today, Abby?'

Again, Abby is unperturbed by this new stranger wanting to know her business. She tells her all about her adventures in the city and how she was chasing the baddies, 'who were chasing Abby, but we rescue her and eat crisps!' she finishes triumphantly. I notice that there are at least six empty packets of cheese and onion crisps strewn across the garden.

I watch Jane, as she in turn observes Abby shaking her hands and flapping her arms. She walks ahead of Abby and picks up a ball. 'How are your catching skills, Abby?'

Abby doesn't answer, but stands still and holds out her arms for the throw. When it comes, she misses completely – even though she is poised and ready. She runs off laughing. Jane turns back to us. 'I think that doctor is absolutely right.'

Together we return to the kitchen, leaving Abby to further adventures 'in the city'. Nobody voices the obvious question: what on earth are we going to do?

At the front door, Jane offers the usual platitudes. 'I'll get back to you as soon as I hear anything,' and, 'Call me if you need anything.'

I nod and smile and make the appropriate noises in return. Just at the last minute she grips my arm and really looks into my eyes. 'I know this isn't going to be easy, Louise, but stay strong. Keep going. We'll get there.'

And though I hardly know this woman, somehow I am nodding and believing her.

I see Jane out and walk back in to find Lloyd looking glumly down at his phone. I look at him questioningly.

'I've just got stacks to do. I had better crack on.'

He disappears back to his office, while I head back out into the garden to find Abby.

Who is no longer there.

I look and look and can't see her anywhere, until suddenly I can. She is edging her way out onto the shed roof.

She stands right at the top, holds out her arms in front of her and starts shouting. But it doesn't sound like anything I recognise, anything intelligible. And suddenly I realise what that Darth Vader costume reminds me of, and why I have had a nagging worry about it at the back of my mind, beyond the tomboyishness of it. She looks just like a little priest, preaching a sermon.

Whilst I am very worried about her safety on top of the shed, I also find myself hoping that this little performance has not been witnessed by the neighbours, or anyone in the street.

One of the locals is more than a little bit of a grump and has revealed her views on child abuse to be – how shall we best put this? – not quite in accordance with mine. When Jimmy Saville's victims were coming forward, she told me in her forthright way, 'They're making it up – and if they're not, then they should get over it.'

Unsurprisingly, this neighbour and I have never become best friends. It *may* have been her who has called the police in the past about some of our foster children; I know she thinks they're naughty and that we as a family are 'dragging down the area'. This will add fuel to her fire, I'm sure. We will have to wait and see. But right now I need to get this child down from the shed roof.

'Hi Abby, is it time for hot chocolate and a biscuit?'

The lure works and she begins to climb back down.

Patiently I explain why it is that she shouldn't go back up there again. 'It's dangerous. You could slip and hurt yourself. We are trying to look after you and keep you safe.'

But Abby isn't listening. I can tell by the look in her eyes that she is far, far away. On to the next thought. I am learning that listening isn't really something that Abby does.

I wait until she has finished her chocolate and then try a different tack.

'Would you like to come to the park with the dogs?'

She loves this idea.

We pass Lloyd, who has returned to the kitchen to make another coffee. 'That's a good plan, you'll enjoy that. Now, Abby, why don't you take off your… lovely outfit, so that you don't damage it.'

Decoding that statement, I know that he is really saying, 'Please don't wear that to the park; you look a sight and I find your appearance a little bit disturbing.'

Abby does remove the dark robe, but retains the mask. It's a start.

I hold the dog leads, and find myself holding Abby's hand. I almost don't know how this has happened. I do not take her hand at any point; she seeks mine. Generally I try to avoid imposing myself on a child unless we are near a road, and then I might just take their hand or sleeve if I sense danger from cars. But she holds my hand tightly and repeats, 'I love you, I love you.'

I ask her my name. She giggles and gives a quick wrist click for good measure.

'Wendy!'

Before I have time to reply, she says, 'No-oo-oo. I'm joking. You're Louise. I know that.' She seems to find this hysterical. I am less amused, but fascinated by where this name thing has come from, and what kind of kick she is getting out of it.

As we get to the park I see the usual suspects, fellow dog-walkers, all friends: four elderly men and their dogs.

Each are happily in their eighties and we are long-term park buddies. On a normal day I walk round with them and chew the fat about politics, life, baking cakes (they all bake cakes and grow their own vegetables) and life's irks. A favourite topic is them ribbing me about when I got my speeding ticket and had to do the speed awareness day. They are always in the know about where every roaming speed camera is sitting out of the back of a police van. I really value this information – it's saving me a fortune. I say hello and they all look at Abby with a chorus of variations on 'Hello young lady!'

In response, she runs off around the field with her mask on, looking as far removed from a 'lady' as it is possible to be. They are all fathers and grandfathers and know that we foster. Jerry, who has a whippet named Sophie (I tend to know the dog names better than their owners, truth be told) laughs and looks at me.

'You've got your hands full, there. She's not all there, is she?'

I don't know what the children's social services would say about the use of that phrase to describe her developmental delays, but he is a couple of generations away from me and I guess he is right on some level.

He throws a tennis ball for Sophie, who stretches out to chase it.

There is a zip wire at the end of the field. Abby's head does not even come up to the height of the seat, she is so small. But that seems to matter very little to her, because the next thing I see is that she's jumped up on the seat and has launched herself off, laughing and shouting and kicking her legs.

'Well, would you look at that! Lively little thing, isn't she?

I tell my friends that we think she has Foetal Alcohol Syndrome and explain a little about what FAS is, and what the long-term implications of the condition are. They shake their heads at that, and make the right sympathetic noises.

'Shame. Poor little mite.'

Then John, who is very tall and has a Red Setter, says, 'But what's going to happen to her? She can't stay with you?'

Although it sounds as though there is a question mark on the end, it feels more like a statement of fact. I am amazed that he is so harsh and direct, but in my heart I know that he is right. I explain how the social worker didn't tell us about her conditions and that she was brought from the other side of the country with very little information on her file. There is more collective headshaking and tutting.

'Terrible.'

Meanwhile Abby is still flying around on the zip wire, shrieking and battling some unseen foe as she goes.

The walk continues round the park. Abby checks in every now and then by running at me full-throttle, throwing her arms around me and telling me that she loves me. My dog-walking friends watch this performance with interest. She runs backwards and forwards so many times that there cannot be an ounce of energy left in that little body.

As we prepare to depart the park, Jerry, John and the others all make a fuss of Abby. They are good people. We turn and head back to the path that leads up the gentle hill to my road. I am momentarily distracted by putting dog-poo bags into the purpose-built red bin on the corner when I hear a yelp of pain. I look up to see an old man holding his head, and little Abby holding a big stone, ready to launch what must be another missile at the man. How have we arrived in this situation? I only took my eye off her for just a few seconds.

He is clearly hurt – and evidently quite angry. Here we go. I need that sign again: *Sorry, she's my foster child. She is suffering from trauma and neglect; please be understanding.*

But it is difficult to be understanding when you have been hit on the head. He is very upset and launches into a shouty tirade.

'I am so very, very sorry. I don't know what to say. She is a foster child who has only come to live with us in the last few days. I didn't see her pick up the stone. I am so terribly sorry.' I help him over to a bench and stay with him for a bit until he feels better, and I offer to walk him home.

It is only when he stands that I notice the dog-collar beneath the coat. He must be a vicar. His Christian compassion returns from wherever it momentarily disappeared to. 'Don't worry. I can see that you've got your hands full.'

As he turns to leave he can't resist a parting shot. 'I'll be alright – but *you*, young lady, should not go around hurting people.'

Abby looks genuinely puzzled. She really has no sense of what she has just done wrong. How can her moral compass be so skewed that the very idea that you shouldn't hurt people seems alien to her?

Now I do take her by the hand as we walk up the hill, all the while explaining why she can't behave like that.

'Don't you think it would hurt if *you* were hit by a stone?'

She skips and laughs and does not listen to me. I am wasting my breath, I know I am. There is nothing going on behind her eyes. Nothing is getting through. Nothing.

I watch her, see that she is happy for a moment as she capers along the path, and echo the question from my dog-walking friends. What *is* going to happen to her? What will her destiny be?

Chapter 8

In the evening I sit down to log the day's events, and reflect on the last couple of days. I am beginning to notice that the other children are not engaging with Abby. Usually they enjoy playing with new children – especially Lily, who naturally offers herself up as a mentor to any new child.

It is time to get their thoughts.

Vincent is in the sitting room with the iPad, by himself. Abby, of course, is whizzing round the garden dressed as Darth Vader. Or a priest.

'Are you okay?'

'Yeah, mum.'

But I detect a note of despondency, and an invitation to push.

'Vincent, are you sure?'

There is only a moment's hesitation before he says, 'Well, it's Abby. I don't like her.'

Straight away I feel sad. I feel sorry for Abby. I feel a failure as a mother for having a child that doesn't like another child.

But most of all I feel guilt for bringing into our home a child that he cannot connect with.

'Can you tell me what it is about Abby that you don't like?'

There is a slightly longer pause this time.

'I think… that it doesn't feel safe.'

This makes me gulp.

'I know she's only six and she's very little,' he continues, 'but I just don't feel like everything's okay when she's around.'

I put my arm around him, give him a hug, kiss him on the head. 'Thanks, lovely. I'm sorry.'

He gives a version of his usual pragmatic response.

'It's okay, Mum. It's not your fault.'

But it is, I think. It is my fault, for letting this situation happen.

Lily floats out of the bathroom shortly after. Her hair is wrapped turban-style in a towel. I taught her how to do this when she first arrived with us a few years ago. Now she does it beautifully. I am struck, suddenly, by how much older she looks. And how lovely.

'Can I have a chat?' I ask.

'Is this about Abby?'

Lily is always right on the nail. She has an admirable forthrightness, and is never slow in coming forward. I sometimes imagine her future as a lawyer or headmistress. Never mind that this month's plan is that she will be an interior designer.

'Yes. I want to know what you think. I have noticed that you all stay away from her. And that's not like you.'

Lily needs no further invitation.

'She's horrible. I don't trust her. I know she's been in my room touching things and I think she did this.' She points to a clay owl made at school last term.

It is broken into pieces lying all over the floor. I know for certain that it was set back on her desk and perfectly safe this morning. I noticed it when I was gathering clothes for the wash. And now I feel terrible.

Last is Jackson. If anyone is going to say it how it is, it's Jackson. We began to call him the Bear when he was at nursery. Even then he was taller and bigger than the other children. He has a thick-set body, and a solid determination to match. He and rugby were made for each other. He is a 'tight-head'. I didn't know a single thing about rugby until he joined the town club; now I go to matches virtually every weekend through the season, and even find myself watching it on TV – usually in horror as they jump on each other. Pitch-side, I watch him laugh and shout out instructions to the players, directing his team. He is a big strong boy, but that rough exterior masks a far softer core: he has always been kind and caring underneath.

I knock on his door. He is sitting in his gaming chair with his bear rug across his knees, twiddling buttons and controls furiously. I walk in and smile, giving him a moment to transition between his virtual world and this one. He takes off his headphones when he sees me.

'You okay, Mum?'

I sit on the end of the bed near his chair and look directly at him. 'I'm fine. I just wanted to know how you feel about Abby being here?'

Jackson looks first at the TV. He turns the screen off very deliberately before he speaks. 'I hate her. When's she going?'

I was expecting forthright, but even so, this takes me by surprise. 'Can you tell me why you feel like that?'

'Where do you want me to start? I don't trust her. She lies. She keeps coming in my room. You wouldn't notice, because as soon as you walk upstairs she goes. I can't really explain it. I don't know any other way to say this, Mum. She's a freak.'

Well, I asked. And now I have a pretty good idea about what they all think of Abby. They have never reacted like this before, and we have looked after some incredibly traumatised children with pretty unusual behaviours. But there is just something about Abby. Something unsettling. Clearly we all feel it. I wasn't aware that it was quite as bad as they have just articulated, but I have a responsibility to listen to them.

I walk down to Lloyd's studio. He's busy working on the computer, putting the finishing touches to something for a client. There is a 90s post-Britpop melody streaming melancholically from the speakers. It seems strangely fitting for my mood.

I sit down on the other desk chair and tell him what the children have just said.

He stops what he's doing immediately, and looks at me. 'Abby *is* a strange child, Louise. There's no denying it. We can all see it. You can, too. I think she makes them feel uncomfortable. We know that she has a lot going on, but I share their concerns. I'm worried about how long Abby is going to stay, too. We still haven't heard from her new social worker. And how long has that been now? You've said it yourself. It just feels like they've dumped her.'

I can't do anything else for the moment, so I cook. When I call them all down for dinner, Abby has placed her little mahogany chair next to Jackson, who does not seem that impressed with the arrangement. He gives me a little look that says, 'See?' and I return it with a warning smile. I put the lasagne on the table along with a bowl of salad and some garlic bread. The children sit patiently, chatting about this and that, the trials and tribulations of the day.

I watch and listen as Abby talks above them all, never stopping to listen to what anyone else is saying. Never stopping for breath. Never actually interacting. Her volume button is set way too high. I wonder if she just wants to join in and be friends, but needs some help with how to go about it. I have no idea how she has got on at school in the past, as I haven't received any of that paperwork; but that's where so much socialising happens for children, so I wonder.

I don't know what mealtimes were like for her at home. We have looked after so many children who never had the equivalent of a mealtime; they just ate something when

174

they were hungry. Usually nothing healthy. Abby does look more at home sitting around a table, and I know that she has siblings, so perhaps she is familiar with this kind of set-up. Though I can't be sure – her manners still leave an awful lot to be desired and her default setting is to chew in the most ungainly way.

Jackson reaches into the lasagne with the big serving spoon. As he lifts the portion back to his plate, Abby knocks his arm and Jackson drops it all on the table. I witness it all as if in slow motion. Abby's actions, though often clumsy and uncontrolled, seem entirely deliberate in this moment.

Jackson has now moved beyond being unimpressed, and I quickly step in before he can react.

'Actually, Abby, you need to sit over here.' I take out another chair and nudge her along the table so that she can't easily reach Jackson. I pull a load of pieces of kitchen paper from the roll and clear it all up – an acknowledgement to Jackson that it wasn't his fault. I scoop another portion out for Jackson – and then do the same for each of them. I feel a reluctance to put that serving spoon anywhere near Abby.

I put a portion onto her plate.

She points at the garlic bread. 'That! THAT! I love that!' she exclaims.

Jackson, who has already had more than enough, turns round to her challengingly.

'You do, do you? What is it, then?'

Abby's reply surprises us all. 'Ice cream.'

The way she says it makes me think that she really believes what she is saying. That this is indeed ice cream.

It dawns on me, suddenly, that she does not know what any of the food is that she is eating. And while I can't explain exactly why, it feels a bit like when she called me Wendy. It's weird, a little off-beat. I break a piece off and put it on her plate. 'Try it.'

'Mmmmmmm, I love this, Wendy.'

Jackson laughs and says, under his breath, but loud enough for us all to hear, 'Dumb ass.'

Abby spits the garlic bread at Jackson.

'Right!' I feel as if I might have a full-on food-fight on my hands if I am not careful. 'That will DO!' I regain my calm, momentarily. 'Please do not behave like that at the table.'

Her response is, by now, predictable. She laughs, gives the rattly little giggle that is so characteristic, and adds the wrist-clicking percussion for good measure. She starts jumping around in her seat.

I take a deep breath and seek my inner yogini. When the zen has returned, I plan for the future. I can't salvage this meal, but tomorrow I will place Abby at the end of the table and dish her food up, cutting it into pieces so she doesn't shovel it into her mouth and spit it out so easily. My plans are all very well, but now that I know how the children feel about Abby, I feel deeply sad. There is nothing worse than knowing that your children are unhappy in their own home. It's an impossible situation. I need to do something, and soon, and I have no idea what.

I clear away dinner and send the children off to do their homework. I sit with Abby at the kitchen table, along with a pile of printing paper and felt tips.

'Would you like to do some drawing?'

She smiles, then laughs, in her customary way. 'I love drawing!'

That's good, then. I continue to busy myself tidying up while she draws on the paper. Often a child might say, 'What shall I draw?' I'll pluck an idea out of the air and they will disagree and do something else. Abby doesn't do this. She selects some colours: yellow, red and the ubiquitous black. Firstly she covers the page with loose movements of the yellow, then throws the pen to the side and layers the page in tight thick lines of black.

'Wendy, look,' she demands, holding the paper up.

I remind her that my name is Louise and say, 'That's interesting, Abby. What's going on in your picture?'

She doesn't explain, but picks up the red felt tip and dots colour across the page with it, so now there are black lines interspersed with red blobs.

Suddenly she stops, gets down from the table and runs from the room. 'I need a poo,' she calls from the door as she flies off.

I can't really make any sense of her picture, but there is something alarming and quite sinister about it. The yellow seems like happier thoughts, happier times. Maybe to do with mum and brother, who she seems to have adored. The heavy black lines have cancelled out the yellow. Something bad happening to erase the sunshine. What is the red? Blood? Pain? I don't know. Perhaps I am reading too much into this. It disturbs me enough that I decide to keep it to show the social worker whenever he or she eventually turns up.

I want to get hold of Abby to give her the dose of antihistamine. I go upstairs to look for her. There she is, larking about outside Jackson's door; she hasn't seen me.

She is standing in his doorway doing a silly dance and singing out, 'You've got a small weenie, you've got a small weenie.'

I call out to her to come away from Jackson's door. She just blows raspberries back at me and sticks her tongue out before running past me down the corridor doing a passable impression of a wild banshee.

This isn't going to go down as one of my greatest foster-parenting days, but there remains some icing on the cake, so to speak.

I go in to Abby's room to gather her pyjamas ready for a bath, and I'm hit by a horrid smell. I see almost instantly that she has pooed into the bedroom bin.

Eventually I manage to create the illusion of some semblance of order upstairs. I cajole the other children into helping me by pretending to go to bed at the same time as Abby. They head to their rooms, calling out, 'Goodnight Jackson!' 'Goodnight Lily!' 'Goodnight Vincent!' 'Goodnight Abby!' 'Goodnight everyone!' like we are in some sort of warped episode of *The Waltons*. I just about stop myself from saying 'Goodnight Jim-Bob' and give them whispered promises that they can then sneak back down, once Abby is settled, for some more television. They quite enjoy the collusion, the fact that we are in this together. It's a little spirit of the Blitz. Abby joins in all the good-nighting. And it seems to work. We are just settling into a nice episode of *Only Fools and Horses*, when Abby appears at the door, eyes wide at our deception.

Ploy failed, I send the kids off to bed for real.

It takes another hour before Abby is really settled. Lloyd and I sit with a nice glass of wine working out the next phase of our strategy for dealing with Abby. I am torn between wanting privacy from the door being closed and needing it ajar to listen out for the next drama. It is still only the first week of Abby being with us. Her arrival has been like a tornado tearing through the house. I am utterly exhausted, and so is he.

Mealtimes and bedtimes are the top priority. And I could do without a repeat of poo-gate.

'The antihistamine is pointless. Whatever the doctor says, it has no effect.' Lloyd takes a sip from his glass.

'You're right. Last night she was doing handstands in her room until the small hours. No matter how many times I went in to try and put her back to bed, she kept getting up. It's alright for you, you managed to fall asleep through all the racket.'

I pause. It's not Lloyd's fault that he managed to sleep when I couldn't. 'But even when I did finally hear her stop and waited a little while to be sure before checking on her, it was two thirty in the morning. And then I was awake thinking about her until she woke me up at half past four by charging into our room laughing and bouncing around on the chair in the corner.'

'Yes, I wasn't impressed at that time in the morning.'

'I know. You made that clear. I shooed her out and took her downstairs so that you could go back to sleep.'

It is causing a problem between us as well as for us both, and we go round in circles trying to come up with solutions.

'It's not too late to call Jane,' Lloyd suggests. 'She said you could reach her anytime.'

I dial the number and give her the latest developments.

'I hear you, Louise, but we are still waiting for a response from the Looked-After-Child team.'

'It's not even a week and we are nearly done! She is exhausting and the children don't want her here. Jane, I need to be honest with you. This is turning into a nightmare.'

'Yes, I can see that. We need to speak to her social worker. Believe me, I am as frustrated as you. She starts school next week and that should help. Not only will you have time in the day again, but hopefully she will expend plenty of that energy during the school day and she will get tired.'

I agree, and apologise for my outburst.

Jane laughs. 'We'll get through this. She is a challenging child.'

'What an understatement that is,' I mutter to myself as we end the call.

Chapter 9

During the days that follow before school starts, I decide that I will take Abby out for long walks with the dogs in the woods. We are lucky in that where we live we can access beautiful places within half an hour in the car. I make a picnic lunch and set off with Abby and the dogs. I find a good spot to park up the car and let the dogs out first. I go to Abby's side to help her undo the seatbelt, but she is already out and running about in the grass. I take the lunch bag – I know just the place for sitting and nibbling a sandwich – and head off.

The dogs love coming out on big country walks. They may be little but they are very mighty and seem to visibly grow in the majestic countryside. I watch Abby throw herself around, running and laughing. I notice that she seems much happier outside than in. I begin to wonder again what has happened to her. I am far from an expert, but feel after six years of fostering, and growing up as an abused child in care myself, that I can tune into children – perhaps in ways others can't.

I return to thinking about her room and how she had moved it to resemble her old bedroom. I ponder that strange choice of fancy dress costume, and the rejection of all things pink and princess or unicorn-related. How she seems naturally drawn to anything black and dark. Absolutely the opposite of the usual choices that a young girl might make. Focusing on the colour black makes me think about her drawing, and how the black had covered and ruled out the yellow. I know that I am tempted to see those red dots as blood and pain.

There is no doubt in my mind that she has FAS, even if not yet officially diagnosed. I think about how her brain is functioning and how added into that is trauma. The heavy use of black on the page tells me that someone or something has scared and hurt her. I wonder why she pooed in her room. It seems such an odd thing to do. A few years ago we looked after a boy a little older than Abby who had been sexually abused by his granddad. It had been anal abuse and the boy had to have surgery. I wonder if Abby has been sexually abused. Maybe the drawing triggered a reaction. She dashed off so quickly to do a poo – and then chose to do it in a room that she has moved to look like her old room.

I am no detective, but something is going on here – and I always see children's behaviour as a form of communication.

Why can't we know more about her adoptive family? Why did they relinquish her? And why did all those foster placements break down? Perhaps the last is easier to answer – most people aren't going to take kindly to defecating in bedrooms.

But I learnt a long time ago to take what is said by social workers about placement breakdowns with a pinch of salt. It's frustrating, because if they told the truth we could do a far better job of supporting the child; but their priority is always to get a child placed. It's a tricky one. The whole system is built on non- and not-quite truths.

Abby is still running. She has found a long, chunky stick that I might put in the back of the car later for our log burner. She looks alive and happy. I love to see children outside, with colour in their cheeks – and, for the first time since she arrived, she has colour. That sickly, translucent pale is disappearing. She looks healthier and pretty with a flush of red to her complexion.

We have been walking for about an hour. I find my bench unoccupied: the benefit of being here on a weekday. I call Abby to sit down and have her lunch. The dogs jump up on the bench and sit with us, which amuses Abby. She is having a great day. Dotty is fine with Abby; it's just the children who don't seem to like her. I wonder whether, if I give them more time and she settles down, they will come to like her. We all need time to adjust. Perhaps it is just a matter of time. Out here in the fresh air it all seems manageable. It's just at moments in the middle of the night when I feel like I really can't cope. It's a bit like having a newborn, I tell myself. It will all pass.

I pass her a tin foil parcel of cheese sandwiches. She eats them up. I chat away, point out the amazing view and ask her if she can see this and that.

She turns round to me and very matter-of-factly explains, 'I can't see anything out of this eye.'

'How long has it been like that?' I ask.

'Forever,' is her devastating answer.

'But didn't anyone notice or take you to the doctors?'

She shakes her head.

I look at her eye more closely, then wave my hand about in front of it. There is no movement, no reaction. I remember that when I took Abby to the doctors he did pick something up about vision when he said that he suspected Abby might have a lazy eye.

Abby interrupts my train of thought with an even more shocking revelation. 'Gordon hit me and then I couldn't see.'

If memory serves me correctly, then Gordon was her adoptive mother's first husband, who she had a baby with.

'When did this happen?' I ask.

Abby explains that it happened when Gordon shouted at her. 'Gordon wasn't very nice. He always shouted at me. And hit me.'

Abby seems so lucid that I keep the horrible conversation going even though I want it to stop. 'Do you know what made Gordon angry, Abby?'

'He called me the spawn of Satan and said that I was sick and evil.'

My eyes are watery, and it is not just because of the wind on the hill. The callousness of those words, the damage they must have caused. It beggars belief. 'That's horrible, Abby, and not true. You are *not* those things; you are a little girl who has had a difficult time of it and no adult should ever talk to you like that. It's very, very wrong.'

Abby leans into me and puts her hand with the half-eaten cheese sandwich over my stomach. 'I love you, Wendy.'

'It's Louise, Abby. My name is Louise.'

She giggles and says, 'Silly me.'

We walk for another good hour or so. Abby achieves four or five times the distance as me just by running to and fro. She is safe and carefree out of doors. It is so clear to see that she likes it. Being indoors seems to make her behave so differently. Inside she is edgy and troublesome, while outdoors she is fine. I wonder what has happened indoors to make her behave in the way that she does.

Then I remember about the stone she threw at the vicar yesterday. That was outdoors. Why did she throw the stone? Was it because the target was a man of the cloth? Or because he was older? As we walk along the stoney lane back to the car, I open up another avenue of conversation.

'Have you got a granny and granddad?' I ask.

'Yes. Nanny and Grandpa. Gordon's mum and dad. They're horrible, too.'

That isn't much help. But I am struck by the forceful 'too' on the end of her sentence.

'Do they go to church?'

'All the time,' she says. 'And Gordon.'

There we go, I think. Maybe this is gradually beginning to fall into place.

'Did you go, too? Tell me about it.'

Abby launches into a complicated description of the church. Lots of statues and icons. Where the altar is, how the pews are laid out. It sounds like a Catholic Church to me, but she doesn't say that directly.

'Did you like it?'

'No. Church isn't fun if you are the spawn of Satan.'

The way she says those words gives me the chills.

'But you're not,' I remind her, and change the subject rapidly.

When we get back Lloyd greets us with a warm smile and asks Abby if she had a nice time.

Abby shouts, 'Yes!' at the top of her lungs and then races out into the garden to find the scooter. The mad scooting circles resume.

'Jane called,' Lloyd tells me. 'And there's good news. She has tracked down the new social worker. They are both coming tomorrow at 10am.'

I am mightily relieved. I go to my laptop and begin to write down all the things that Abby told me while we were walking. I'm not entirely convinced about being blind in one eye, but I do think there may be something in the information about Gordon, and perhaps the church. Though

I could also be adding two and two to make five – it's not unknown.

Notes complete, I go back into the kitchen and notice Abby out of the window. She is up on the shed shouting at our next-door neighbour. I dash outside. I can hear Lloyd's chair on the floor in his studio and his door swinging open. He is coming out too.

Running to the bottom of the garden, I tell Abby to get down.

She responds with an emphatic, 'No!'

'Abby, you really need to get down here now or you will hurt yourself.'

'But I can see everyone from up here,' she calls. 'And I like it!'

The neighbour, whose patience has clearly been tried already, says, 'I'm afraid she just called my husband a...' here she breaks off to a whisper, 'nosy bastard'.

This is outrageous behaviour, and I have no wish to upset my neighbours.

'Abby, it is not okay to talk to people like that!' I call, but even I can hear how ineffectual it sounds.

Lloyd has his hands firmly planted on his hips and has come out to the bottom of the shed. His body language tells me that he is very cross. 'Abby. Will you get yourself down here, now.' It is a statement, not a question.

There is clearly something about the loud tone of a man's voice that she responds to, because Abby capitulates immediately, flies down the side of the shed, rolls onto the ground and darts off.

I look at Lloyd, who knows I don't approve of shouting (even though on a few occasions I have shouted myself). But there is no denying that it has had the desired effect in the heat of this moment. He shrugs and returns to his studio.

Abby has fled to her room. She has a packet of felt-tips, given by me – perhaps somewhat foolishly. Though, after the antics of another foster child with permanent marker all over her room, I tend to avoid anything that won't easily scrub away. Abby is lying on the floor, drawing. I sit on the chair and lean in to look at the rows and rows of black circles. As an artist I find them interesting, but as a foster carer I find them deeply troubling.

'What are you drawing?'

'Me.'

I think about this for a moment. I have seen her rip up paper into tiny pieces before – that first night with the book. This feels the same. Does it represent how she feels about herself? Does she feel that she is tiny pieces and little circles?

The red dots appear again on the page.

'What are the red dots?'

She stays absolutely focused on the paper, but answers, 'My bum.'

This isn't what I was expecting at all.

I swallow and asks what she means.

She rolls over to face me, lifts a leg into the air and points at her bottom. 'My bum. The other one hurt it.'

The other one? I need to be careful now. I need to make absolutely sure that I am not putting words or ideas into her mind, suggesting anything. She needs to tell me herself, in her own words.

'Oh, Abby. I am so sorry to hear this. Can you tell me more?'

She rolls back to the drawing and makes thick black marks across the page once more. The image takes on a depressing familiarity to the previous sketch she did.

Aside from the language itself, I am interested as to why she called our neighbour a nosy bastard.

'Do you miss any of them? Your nanny and grandpa, Gordon, the other one?'

She draws intently. 'No. I don't. I hate them, and they hate me. They said I was made from bad things.'

'Oh, Abby. That really isn't true. You are made from all the same things as everyone else. You are a little person, no different from any other person.'

She turns her head to me. 'What, like you?'

'Just like me,' I smile.

She jumps up from the floor and gives me a giant hug, kissing my face. 'I love you, Louise.'

It is lovely that she says that and reacts in that way, but I am still uncomfortable with it. She has only known me for less than a week, after all. But I am learning more about her. I think she is deeply traumatised and abused, in every way. She is so young to have to deal with this. I have no idea about her education – where she is in real terms, what age she is functioning at. It is definitely way below her chronological age, but I don't know how far behind. All I know is that this child has been severely let down by her adults, all of them – including social workers, back where she came from. It makes dealing with all her behaviours bearable. I ask Abby if she would like to come downstairs to have a drink. She jumps up and grabs hold of my hand, giggling all the while.

In the kitchen I start preparing dinner. I also keep thinking about all the things Abby has told me. As she sits at the table sipping on her hot chocolate, I ignore the unpleasant slurping noises and ask her what her favourite colour is. I expect the answer to be 'black', but to my surprise she answers, 'yellow'.

'But I thought you loved black?'

She looks at me and says, 'I do.'

'Why?'

'Because it is the colour of a cassock.' She takes another sip from her mug.

I don't know quite what a cassock is, but it sounds like something to do with the church. And it doesn't sound like the answer that a six-year-old should be giving.

Before I have a chance to pursue this she says, 'But I love yellow too. Because it is the colour of Mummy's hair.'

Bingo! There we are, I think. She loves her mum. I knew it. I feel that I can push a bit more. 'Was Mummy kind?'

'Oh, Yes. Mummy stopped Daddy from hurting me.'

I hold my breath, say nothing.

'Daddy hit me and punched me when I needed punishing.'

Abby does a pretend punch to her chin and gives it a horrible crunching sound effect. The idea that a six-year-old, an innocent, would 'need punishing' is also chilling.

'That's a wrong way to behave, Abby. Your Daddy was very bad to do that. Did he hurt you in other ways?'

Abby shakes her head, 'Only hitting.'

I'm glad, but that forlorn 'only' gets me.

Then she does a strange thing. She gets onto her knees on the chair, bends over and points at her bottom. 'The other one did that.'

She carries on calmly sipping her drink. I need to know who this 'other one' is. A priest? I have to confess that I am thinking about all the worst things I have ever heard about the Catholic Church.

'The other one?' I question. But Abby shakes her head.

I mentally track back over the conversations we have had, and the notes that I have read. I don't think that she has mentioned another name before. Sometimes being a foster carer is so hard. You can learn some terrible things and not know where to go with it. I know foster carers sometimes get cross when fellow professionals talk about therapy for social workers and educational psychologists after they have worked closely with a child who has been abused. It's recognised that they need support. It can be deeply, deeply upsetting for anyone to hear and deal with this stuff. Unless, of course, you're a foster carer: then you just have to get on with it.

So there is another abuser in the background. This poor kid. I don't think I can take any more. 'Shall we stop talking about it?'

She nods and swallows another mouthful of hot chocolate.

'Well, whoever it was, he was very, very bad to do that, too.'

The words seem so inadequate to explain what has happened to her. I never know with younger children if they feel less burdened after talking about what has happened to them. I also need to bear in mind that Abby is functioning at an emotional age that is different from her chronological age, and has the added factor of FAS.

But I start wondering about her adoptive family once more. She loves her mum. She hates her father. Did her mother have any idea of what the father was doing to her with these 'punishments'? I wonder if her adoptive parents split up *because* her mum knew what the father was doing to Abby. Maybe she wanted to protect Abby and her new baby.

Who is the second abuser? Was 'the other one' after? Because if so, then it sounds as though it might have been a case of out of the frying pan and into the fire – substituting one form of abuse for another. What a start in life. No wonder Abby is confused about people and who to love.

She needs an emotional and moral reset. I need to talk this through with her new social worker tomorrow.

I dish up dinner, carefully placing Abby at the end of the table out of reach of the other children's food. I do my best to keep the children chatting and occupied in their thoughts, encouraging them to tell jokes instead of feeling cross. I don't think I could bear it if any of them were mean to her after what she has just revealed. But they are all playful and light-hearted and that is both a relief and a comfort.

Lily asks for ice cream for pudding. I ask Abby if she would like some, too.

She smiles and says, 'I love ice cream.'

I gather four bowls and ask Vincent to get the chocolate and strawberry sauce from the cupboard – which he happily does. I carefully measure out three scoops of vanilla ice cream into each bowl. They all happily chat away. I walk to the other end of the table with the sauces and ask which one Abby would like.

'Strawberry.' I give her the jar and watch her as she squeezes the contents on her ice cream. I suggest she stops as she now has more sauce than ice cream. She laughs, gives a little wrist-click and keeps going. I gently take the sauce away and ask her why she needs so much sauce.

'I don't want to see the ice cream.'

This resonates with other things that she has said. In her drawings she covers the earlier image up: the yellow, the round marks. She seems to repeat this pattern of covering up and I find it interesting.

After dinner the children are soon off doing their various bits and pieces. Abby asks if she can have a bath on her own tonight, without me there. I am more than a little hesitant, as I never quite know what she's going to do. I agree – she has offloaded plenty today and deserves some time alone – but I ask her to wait while I load the dishwasher up. 'I want to see how much water is going into the bath.'

She laughs, 'Alright, then,' and quietly slips away from the kitchen. I just make the assumption that she is going upstairs, and that the worst that might happen is that she begins running the bath even though I have asked her not to. I shut the dishwasher door – and hear Vincent crying. I move quickly, as does Lloyd from his studio, into the sitting room. A gruesome scene greets us: Vincent is lying on the floor in the sitting room, holding his head. There is blood all over his hands. Abby is standing on the sofa with her hands over her mouth. What on earth is going on? I run straight to Vincent who is very upset, and in some pain. He tells us that Abby suddenly appeared while he was standing near the TV playing with the Wii.

'Out of nowhere. I didn't even know she was there. She picked up the remote control and whacked me really hard on the head, then kicked the back of my legs so that I fell onto the TV table and smashed my head on the corner.

I thought at first it was his hands, but his head is indeed bleeding.

Abby, bouncing on the sofa, laughs. 'I don't know what he's talking about! I didn't do anything!'

I sit Vincent up and check him over. It is a nasty little cut, though thankfully the bleeding looks to be stopping. I want to see if he has concussion. He can stand up, but is very wobbly on his feet. He describes seeing stars and tells me that he feels sick.

I don't know quite what to do about Abby. It is the utter lack of remorse or empathy that is so disturbing. I am in a bit of a maternal panic over Vincent, and Lloyd is very cross. Jackson and Lily now arrive at the door to the sitting room.

'What's she done now?' This from Jackson, who then rushes up to his brother, puts his arm around him and asks him again what has happened. 'What did she do?' There is no question in his mind that this is some sort of accident. The assumption is that Abby has caused it.

I feel useless. What sort of mother am I that I can't keep my own son safe in our house?

Jackson looks at me, then at Abby, still bouncing on the sofa, and back to me. 'Mum, she has to go.'

I feel sick.

Lloyd asks Abby to get down from the furniture and put her pyjamas on.

Abby does indeed get down from the sofa, but skips around the room shouting, 'No, Fatty!'

I decide that I need to take Vincent to A&E to get checked over; he is still holding his head. I ask Jackson to come with us.

Lily asks if she can come too. 'I don't want to stay here with her!'

I bundle my injured child and his siblings into the car and drive to the hospital, feeling utterly awful. Whatever has happened to Abby, I can't allow the safety of my children to be compromised. What am I *doing*?

Vincent is fine. He has a little concussion, as I suspected, but the doctor is happy for him to come home. When the doctor asks Vincent what happened and I listen to Vincent, my kind, quiet boy, tell the doctor about Abby, I cry.

'Oh – what I have I done?' It comes out as a half-sob, half-wail.

The doctor is sympathetic. 'Sometimes it's not easy, is it? Fostering.'

I shake my head.

On the way home I decide on impulse to swing into McDonald's. I am amazed that they can all find space to eat a full-size Meal Deal and wash it down with a McFlurry. Whatever else has happened, appetites have not been damaged.

It is 10pm before we finally get home. As soon as we get through the front door I can hear Lloyd asking Abby to stay in bed. I need to get the other three to bed – they have school in the morning. Jackson looks at me and in a low voice says, 'Get rid of her.'

Lily looks at me with pleading eyes. 'Please, Louise. She's horrible.'

Vincent, with his bandaged head, doesn't need to say anything. I know what he must be thinking. I tell them all to get ready for bed.

Lily suddenly comes back out into the hall in tears.

'What's wrong?'

She holds out the figure that her birth mother made her from clay. Like the pottery owl, it is now broken into several pieces. I know that she kept it on the middle shelf in a glass cabinet in her room, up out of the way and protected because it was important to her and was meant to be safe.

Lloyd says to Abby in a stern voice that I rarely hear, 'You are *not* to go in their rooms. At all. Under any circumstances. Do you hear me? You know this!'

Abby just laughs and begins swinging her bedroom door backwards and forwards, open and shut, over and over again. Lloyd gives me a look that I recognise. This is my fault. It is a look that makes me feel terrible.

Abby eventually goes to bed at 2am. I stay up until then, for the safety of the rest of us, as well as to look after her. My respite is short. She wakes up and is running up and down the hallway by 5am.

I shoo her downstairs so as not to wake up the others after what was also a late night for them. I get my laptop and tap in everything that has happened. I am in a strange mood. I have a child in my home who is turning our lives

198

upside down – and making my children feel fear in their own home. I have to listen to the children. I have to be sure that I am protecting them. Abby may be small, but she is extremely powerful and manipulative – and I have a horrible premonition that she has not even really got going yet.

Chapter 10

After the children have gone to school – all reminding me that they want Abby to go – I prepare for the meeting with the social worker. The house is, frankly, after everything that has happened, a bit of a mess. I run round sorting it out, putting shoes away, cushions back on the sofa and the breakfast debris in the dishwasher. I check the clock to see if I have time to walk the dogs before the scheduled arrival time of 10am.

I bomb down the lane to the park. No one is there apart from tall John and his little white dog. He takes one look at me, dispenses with ordinary greetings, and asks, 'How's it going with Abby?'

As we walk around the park I pour out all the horrors of the last few days. It's a relief to let it all out.

He quietly listens and just before I go back up the lane he says, 'You can't help everyone. Don't feel guilty because you feel that you need to protect your family.'

'But what about Abby? What will happen to Abby?'

'I know that it's hard, but they should never have put her with you, never have put all that emotional strain on you and your family. Perhaps she needs something else.'

I love my over-eighties counselling sessions from the park. Walking home I feel less guilty and a little more pragmatic. When I left, Abby was playing in the garden, outside, of course. We have moved anything that she could have climbed on to get on top of the shed, so I am fairly confident that she can't be back up there – but I can't see any sign of her. I look everywhere, calling out her name. Finally I find her inside the shed. She is sitting in her black robe – a cassock? – amongst the parasols and lawn mower with a pile of crisps and biscuits, and a hoard of stolen items from the house. There are some tubes of paint from my studio, containers from the bathroom, toys from the other children's bedrooms. It is a fair old treasure trove. Somehow I resist the temptation to be cross. There isn't time.

I tell Abby that her new social worker will be here soon to say hello, and that Jane is coming along too. She doesn't seem that fussed, but comes into the house. Knowing what these meetings are like of old, I explain that when the adults get boring she can watch a film. She picks an animated one from the pile and I get it all set up, ready to go. I give strict instructions about how she is not to touch the technology.

The door goes a good few minutes before I am expecting it to. It's Jane.

'I hope you don't mind; I thought I would get here five minutes early just so we are ready.'

I ask if Jane knows the social worker.

'No, not personally. But I do know that she has recently come back from maternity leave – oh, and she is part-time.'

Already I don't like what she is telling me. A part-time social worker is a problem when you have a placement as demanding as Abby and are likely to need regular input. Lily's social worker only sees her every three months because Lily is happily settled – but Abby is another kettle of fish. Why don't the people in charge of allocating cases think these things through?

The door goes again and I leave Abby chatting with Jane. She is relaxed in Jane's company and I notice that Jane, in turn, talks to her clearly and gently – with very deliberately just one question at a time. I think her mind can process this better, and make a mental note to follow Jane's lead on this.

I go to the door. Standing on the doorstep is our new social worker, who introduces herself as 'Tiger Lily'. I think that even if Jane hadn't told me she was recently returned from maternity leave, I could have guessed; she has her hair scraped back from her face in what I can only describe as a 'new mum' ponytail, and her clothes sit ill on her, as though she is adjusting to a new body shape. She has a strong Welsh accent that I love, though. I am fascinated by accents, although of course I believe myself not to have one. (Lloyd picks me up on h-dropping; I'm fond of 'ello as a greeting, or inviting people into the 'ouse, but I am in good company: watching Radiohead at Glastonbury on the TV a few years ago, we noticed that Thom Yorke dropped his 'h's too. I sat there laughing. So I don't have an accent as such; I just choose to use the letter 'h' intermittently.)

But Tiger Lily seems nice and offers a warm smile as she enters. She does speak to me a bit like I am a child, but that may be because she has had recently had a baby and has been lacking in adult time. I remember what that is like. I forgive her.

Lloyd comes into the kitchen and shakes Tiger Lily's hand, managing to suppress any kind of response to her name as she is introduced. I ask her if she would like a drink, and she asks if I have herbal tea. I do. It just takes me a minute to find it. We all sit down, as does Abby on her chosen too-small chair.

Tiger Lily begins by talking directly to Abby. I always have a feeling of inner cringe when I'm at meetings between adults and a child. There is a peculiar pattern common to these kind of interactions with foster children. I watch a child become the centre of everyone's attention and observe how they deal with this. Our Lily, for example, is polite and quiet but she has become more assertive over time. Some children just seek control – and Abby falls into this category. I am not surprised. A child who goes from having nothing – little to no love – can turn into a mini-monster as they soak up the wrong kind of attention. All the adults pile their social guilt, their selectively applied training and their own agendas and ideas onto the child. So I hold back and watch the mistakes being made. But I am careful not to withdraw enough for the social worker to pick up on anything and write it down. I want to avoid a note being made such as: *Louise seems stern or quiet in the meeting, displaying little emotion.* I am now never surprised by their reporting styles.

But I watch Tiger Lily introduce herself to Abby as 'Tortoise Tiger Lily' and make a strange jerky action with her head and neck – a gesture that I can only assume is intended to represent the action of a tortoise sticking its head from a shell. Apparently it is to help Abby remember her name. I would have thought that Tiger Lily was distinctive enough, and introducing a second animal into the equation might only confuse things, but what do I know?

Suddenly I'm 'Lovely Louise'.

I clear my throat. 'It's okay. Actually, I think she has my name.' I say this while desperately hoping that I am no longer 'Wendy' – which might make me look a little foolish in the current circumstances, but the fact is that I am not entirely happy about being referred to as Lovely Louise. Sometimes I have to enforce boundaries and rules, and Abby won't be thinking I'm lovely then. Jane quickly becomes 'Jingle Jane.' I catch her fake smile and find that I almost can't wait to hear what Lloyd is going to be known as. We move on so that Lloyd doesn't get a name, but I will think on that for later. It keeps me amused for the first part of the meeting.

Tortoise Tiger Lily asks Abby how she likes her new home. 'It's good.'

I watch Jane with a degree of curiosity, as somehow I can tell that this is not how she would do things. Eventually Abby does get bored and I take her into the sitting room to watch the film. She has already prepared the camouflage blanket, which I tuck around her. She seems to like that, and it strikes me that maybe the camouflage is part of the hiding and covering-up process for Abby.

While I have been away, Tiger Lily has been listening to the list of events that have taken place since Abby's arrival with us. Jane has clearly read all my emails and logs very thoroughly. I like Jane. I think we have a good supervising social worker here.

I carefully relay Abby's accounts of adults that have hurt her, and tentatively share my theory about her mum; that is, that her adoptive mum loved her and made various efforts to make life better for Abby, such as beginning the investigations for FAS. I suggest that an affinity with her adoptive mother is what she feels, in contrast with a kind of fear for her adoptive father, who seems to have punished her repeatedly. 'And she says that her mum tried to stop the dad from hurting her. I'm even wondering if that might have been what caused the family break-up.'

'We don't know that. I think you might be reading too much into it,' says Tiger Lily. Who clearly knows nothing about anything. I hesitate before I tell her about 'the other one', but I have to report it.

'I'm fearful that she has suffered some kind of sexual abuse as well as the physical punishments. And at the hands of someone else.' I explain how the conversation with Abby developed.

Tiger Lily writes it all down, this time without comment, and Jane neatly brings the conversation round to the plan.

'The biggest thing is that we really need to see the paperwork,' I state. Jane backs me up, explaining that there are big gaps in the paperwork that we do have, and that the missing bits appear to be the most important. We are really in the dark about the history of this child. Perhaps that is why I am 'reading too much into it', I think – but do not say.

I am curious as Tiger Lily leans down to her bag and pulls out a bundle of papers in a big envelope.

'Well. According to these records, Abby was put up for adoption because her birth mother was only 13 years old when she became pregnant by her uncle. The family fell apart and wanted Abby out of their lives. Apparently her mother had drunk significant quantities of alcohol throughout the pregnancy – to the point that her liver became damaged.'

I look at Lloyd and see his eyes soaking up all the information. What an awful story. Jane asks about the adoptive family.

'Soon after they adopted Abby, the mum fell pregnant naturally.'

'As is so often the way,' Jane shares a grim laugh. 'When the pressure of getting pregnant is removed, that's when a couple conceive.'

'So, what happens when a couple has adopted a baby, and then has a birth baby?' I ask.

'Well, that would ultimately depend on where you are,' Jane answers, rather cryptically.

Lloyd frowns. 'Postcode life chances, then.'

We all agree with his assessment.

Tiger Lily goes on to explain, 'In the county where Abby was adopted, at the time of her adoption, they were…'

Jane steps in and cuts her off. 'Throwing babies at people?'

'Um, yes. Those weren't exactly the words I was going to use, but yes. It was quite easy to adopt.'

'And then throwing them away again afterwards, when they'd had enough, or things didn't quite turn out as perfectly as they'd hoped,' I say, with all the bitterness that I feel.

I sit back and think about my own adoption in the late 80s. When I read my file I learnt that it was a 'forced' adoption – against many objections from social workers and guardians. I feel sad. It sounds as though Abby's may just have been too easy. Maybe her adopters should never have been allowed to adopt her in the first place.

Tiger Lily interrupts my thoughts. 'Her adopted parents were deeply religious.'

I laugh out loud at this, and then find myself immediately apologising. I remind everyone about the disclosure from Abby about what she said her adopted dad did to her in terms of punishment. 'Not very Christian, in my book.'

Jane is diplomatic. 'We can't really investigate that, but I will look into it to see if there are any other cases connected to Abby's dad.'

'But why,' I ask, fixing my eyes on Tiger Lily, 'did the social workers not give me any of this information before?'

'Honestly, I don't know. Perhaps they couldn't find it?'

I know this must be rubbish. How do you 'not find' information like this? And then I answer my own question as I remember the circumstances of how Abby arrived with us. Probably quite easily, when you are trying to place a child in an emergency. Unsurprisingly, perhaps, she is protecting the practices of her colleagues, and I don't blame her for that, but make a mental note to examine what she herself says closely. If she is going to cover up for others then perhaps I am not able to trust her completely, either.

Jane tries to keep everything on track. 'So, that looks like the complete handover now. Are we waiting for any more information?'

'As far as I know, Louise now has everything,' Tiger Lily explains.

I ask if I can see the education report, as Abby is starting school on Monday.

There is a moment of riffling through the paperwork before Tiger Lily says, 'Oh. I don't think that's here.' She licks her lips and there is something reptilian about the action. I am beginning to think that 'Tortoise Tiger Lily' wasn't such a bad moniker after all.

I say nothing.

Lloyd cuts to the chase. 'How long is Abby staying with us?'

I know that he is hoping, as indeed I am, that we will hear that it is a month; maybe, at a push, two.

'Umm, she's long term,' Tiger Lily says, and I think that if she did have a shell then her little tortoise head would pop right back in it.

Lloyd is firm. 'No, she is not. Absolutely not. We have never agreed to that. She is a temporary placement and she can't stay here – we can't meet her needs.'

'Are you saying that you are not experienced enough?' Tiger Lily throws back at him, and with sudden clarity I can see where this is going.

Jane intervenes. 'Louise and Lloyd have *not* agreed for Abby to stay long term. I am quite sure they are capable, but they are mainstream foster carers with other children to take care of. Abby is clearly more complex.'

Now Tiger Lily says, as though laying down a challenge, 'But my manager has stated that you are on 'Fostering Plus'. That's the highest payment. Therefore you are expected to be able to look after a child like Abby.'

My first (uncharitable) thought is, '*You cow.*'

Lloyd jumps in before I can voice my thought – with a more pragmatic and peace-making response. 'Regardless of the Fostering Plus status, we have not signed a long-term agreement. Abby came to us as a temporary referral – we signed a short-term placement agreement. Under the circumstances, we would never have signed a long-term agreement.'

She looks back down at her paperwork and insists with some relish, 'Oh, but it appears that you *did* sign the long-term agreement form.'

I get up from the table and go to my office, where I keep my copies of the paperwork. It only takes a few seconds for me to lay my hands on the agreement forms. I know that Lloyd is right. We definitely signed the form entitled 'Temporary'. I experience a moment of relief as I bring it back into the kitchen to show Tiger Lily.

She looks at it and scrunches her forehead. 'There seems to be some mistake.'

I look at Jane, whose face seems to be a mix of thunder and panic. I ask to see the form that Tiger Lily is holding. She tries to put it away.

I insist on seeing the form, and she has little choice but to hand it over.

'Well I'll be… This is a falsified document. Look. You can see where they have changed the header on the photocopier!'

I have the presence of mind to walk off with it to my office to make a copy. My old union training comes in useful, sometimes.

Tiger Lily, having been wrong-footed, is now clearly winging it. 'Well, I will have to take this back to my manager.'

'Yes, you will. And we want a date when Abby will be placed into a setting that is more suited to her needs.' I can feel myself boiling up.

Jane is very quiet, but I don't detect weakness. It is more a sense that she is waiting.

Tiger Lily quickly changes the subject by asking if we are all ready for school on Monday.

My mood has soured but Lloyd says, 'Yes. We are all set. And we hope this helps her settle down.'

I return to an earlier, bypassed subject. 'So, Tiger Lily. What *is* the plan for Abby?'

Jane says, 'We need to have an understanding – today, Tiger Lily – of the short-term plan for Abby. For example, has her case actually got a court date yet?'

Tiger Lily begins to look a bit lost. 'No, I'm afraid that there is nothing in this file that says she is due a court date.'

Lloyd, as always, maintains diplomacy. 'We are happy to help, but we cannot let this drift. We are not the right placement for Abby.'

'Does it say in your bundle why the other placements broke down?' I ask.

Jane leans in, holding her pencil with both hands. Tiger Lily takes on a sheepish expression. 'Well, um, I think that there are a variety of reasons.'

'And what are those reasons?' I persist.

'She, um, well… she didn't always get on with other family members.'

'You mean other children?'

She suddenly finds her sleeve very interesting. 'On occasion.'

Lloyd says, 'I think we need a date, Tiger Lily, don't you? That would be useful.'

'I think I will need to go back to my manager,' is all that Tiger Lily has left. She begins packing up her bag.

Jane just stares.

I walk Tiger Lily to the front door. On our way we walk past the sitting room. She waves at Abby who is buried under the camouflage blanket, but shaking her wrists until they click.

'Are you alright there, Abby?' I ask.

'Yes, Wendy.'

Tiger Lily gives me a quizzical look.

I give an artificial smile and explain, with as much warmth as I can find, 'Oh, don't worry about that. She calls me that sometimes!'

As I say goodbye I reaffirm that we are waiting to hear about a date and a proper plan for Abby.

'Bye then,' she says, not able to get out of the house fast enough.

'Bye Tortoise Tiger Lily,' I say, unable to resist it as a parting shot.

On the way back I say to Abby, 'Why did you call me that? Can you remember my name?'

'Yes, Wendy.'

I say nothing.

When I go back into the kitchen Jane and Lloyd are talking. I blow out my cheeks. 'Well, that was a waste of time, wasn't it?'

'No, not entirely,' Jane says. 'I have some ideas.'

Lloyd sits back with a look that says, 'Louise, get off your high horse, sit down and listen.'

'The good news is,' she continues, 'that by law they have to have a plan and they have to have it in place soon. Also, I will look on our internal system to see if I can find out more about Abby's background. We have a lot more to go on now. I can contact her previous authority but I will have to run that by my manager first.'

'Is your manager as good as Tiger Lily's?' I hear myself say, unconvinced.

'No, she's much better. A proper manager and one who does things by the book.'

'Why do you all do things so differently?' Lloyd is brave enough to ask.

Jane thinks for a moment. 'I think we have inevitably become neo-liberals. Some of us seem to be in this sector for different reasons – but I can assure you that my office is not like hers,' she laughs. 'We are all too old, for one thing.'

Her frankness and self-deprecation breaks the ice that had settled in the room. I laugh too. 'I *had* noticed that the supervising social workers seem to be of a certain age – a little long in the tooth.'

'I hope you aren't comparing me to a horse, my dear!'

'Better than a tortoise!'

Our meeting ends in good-natured laughter, but I can't help but wonder if we are really any further forward.

Chapter 11

The weekend is challenging, to say the least.

Our stressed household is full of arguments. The only way to work it is for Lloyd and me to keep Abby away from the others as much as possible by taking it in turns to take her out. Night-times continue to be difficult for all of us. We have to keep her in our sights the whole time. It is exhausting on top of looking after the others and doing all the jobs you need to do at the weekends. Lloyd and I realise that we will not be going anywhere for some time: a trip to the cinema or nights out are off the agenda for the time being; we are bound to keeping this girl and the rest of our children safe.

I did find time to take Abby to have a look round the school in the previous week. It was a quick tour: thankfully the head was busy and didn't seem to pick up on the undercurrent, or he might not have welcomed us back. I am hopeful about school. A big bit of me wants to think that this is the answer: all that has been missing is her education. She will shine and thrive. But the other bit of me is full of doom and gloom: what if school does not work? What if she is excluded? Was she excluded from her last school? Is that why they have lost the paperwork? It wouldn't surprise me.

I spend a bit of time reading with Abby to try and help her get back into the swing of things. I buy some study books from WH Smith, and to my surprise she seems to enjoy it. She leans in tight and strokes my arm and my face while we are working. She tells me she loves me. For the most part I dismiss what I feel are misplaced affections, but she does say one thing that really makes me think as she strokes my cheek and kisses it. 'You're my favourite.'

Now, I have been doing this work long enough to know that she does not know me well enough to love me. She may well have an attachment to me, but the words bother me. I wonder if someone has told her that she is their favourite, though it seems unlikely, given how unwanted Abby seems to have felt. Certainly she was the odd one out in her adoptive family setup.

My thoughts move to the 'other one'. Perhaps the words came from him, whoever he is. Perhaps they were said before or after he abused Abby. A little shiver shoots down my spine.

I talk in an upbeat manner about school. On Sunday evening, after her bath, I get her to help me lay out her new uniform: shiny black patent leather shoes, a crisp new white polo shirt and a bright red sweat top, a small grey skirt and fresh white ankle socks. I'm a little worried about her rucksack: she chose one in the shape of a storm trooper, rejecting the 'Frozen' bag that I suggested, but it was her choice. Perhaps it is cool. Who am I to know?

Lloyd and I swing from child to child ensuring that they all have time and attention and what they need. I am nervous about tonight. Will she go to sleep before midnight? I don't want her too tired for school. Even though I know and the school knows that she is our foster child, it does not stop me feeling that if she is judged then I will be judged too. If she isn't up to speed they will think I have neglected her education. And if her behaviour is not good I will feel that is my fault too. Even though she has only been here a week I feel that I am totally responsible for every hair on her little head, every aspect of her being. And I will be judged for all of it. I think schools have traditionally had this effect on parents – especially parents who want the best for their children. I also know that not all teachers and classroom assistants understand looked-after children. Not everyone understands attachment and how disorders can impact on a child's self-esteem and behaviour.

Schools as institutions are complex. School still represents a powerful authority that a part of me still hates, and still fears, from my own school days. My education was rather ad hoc due to me being in care; my experience was made far worse as my behaviour was constantly criticised. The 'gift' of dyslexia and dyscalculia that I possess went undiagnosed for many years. As a child I constantly felt anxious at school. And yet I spent over 20 years teaching in higher education.

I know that I won't sleep tonight, whatever Abby's antics. I will be worrying about her and how the school will treat her. I need to be careful not to overlay my anxiety onto her.

But, after everything that has happened, she sleeps in.

'Can you believe it?' I say out loud, several times, to no one in particular. I actually have to go in and wake Abby up at 7am. There is no flying down the hallway and terrorising the banisters today. I put on my biggest grin.

'Good morning, Abby! It's your special day.'

She smiles back in return. I like how this feels so far. I have looked after children that locked themselves in the toilet to avoid going to school. It doesn't seem as though we are to be in that sort of territory, and I am pleased.

The other children seem okay with her this morning, too. Lily asks her very kindly if she is excited – she is – and seeing all of them in the kitchen with their uniform creates a sense of unification that we haven't seen before. I want Abby to feel that she matters, and to belong in the togetherness of family. She seems proud of her uniform and checks her appearance a couple of times in the mirror. I brief all the children not to comment on the rucksack.

Abby and I have a longer walk than the others, whose schools are five minutes' walk from the front door. I hope this is a good opportunity for Abby to get some exercise and focus on her day. When we arrive we go straight to reception. The lady at the desk looks familiar; I recognise her as the mum of one of Lily's friends. She offers us a warm and friendly welcome. So far so good.

Abby begins to flap her arms and then shake her hands so hard that her wrists click again. In my experience of school, the admin staff are usually pretty clued up about children – so I guess she clocks Abby's behaviour. The head teacher soon appears: Mr Brown. He is wearing a high-vis tabard and holding a bell.

He smiles first at Abby and then at me. 'Please take a seat; I will be five minutes.'

We sit down. Abby's eyes are taking in the display board: listed inside the silhouettes of children are word cut-outs promoting the school's values: *Friendliness, Compassion, Delight, Endeavour, Tolerance, Respect.* I wonder if she can read them, let alone understand what they mean, or what they look like in practice. We haven't seen much of those qualities so far. I hope she is okay today. I desperately want her to have a good day.

Mr Brown must be in his late thirties, and prematurely balding, but has the air of a slightly more rotund Mr Chips. He is warm and friendly and instantly interested in Abby. I like that the school seems to be all about the children: adults should come second in this environment. Mr Brown says that he will take Abby to her class, and manages to make Abby giggle.

'Have a good day,' I call, as they head off into the labyrinth of the school corridors together.

To the lady in reception I say, 'Is it okay if I call at lunch-time, just to see how she is?'

'Of course. Talk later.'

I get on with my day, feeling much happier. When I get home, Lloyd is looking at me with an expectant expression.

'She seems happy and went off fine. No problem at all.' I sincerely hope that my optimism is not misplaced. At lunch time I call the school, who report that Abby is having a good day. I sit at my desk and start drawing. Only a week late on this commission! For the first time in a while I can lose myself in the creative work. With illustration, ideas come from the imagination as a set of internal conversations. It feels like a while since I have been able to have them. Work on the drawings feels freeing. I have an energy simply from Abby not being in the house. Time flies by and it isn't long before I find myself ready to meet Abby again outside her classroom at the end of the day.

The teacher, who introduces herself as Miss Jacobs, is a young, plumpish lady who is dressed more like a student than a teacher. She beams at me and comes over. I look at Abby, who seems aglow.

'Wow, you look happy! Did you have a good day?'

'She's done well, today. You can feel really pleased with yourself, Abby.'

I look at the teacher to check that she isn't saying this just for the benefit of Abby. I'm waiting to hear what she broke or destroyed, or who she hurt. But Miss Jacobs just tells me,

'We will do a number of little tests this week just to see where she is and how we can progress.'

I am so happy. I didn't expect day one to go so well. It has been my most productive day for a long time, and it sounds as if it has been for Abby, too. We walk home via the newsagents and I am so impressed that I buy Abby a lolly. I ask her which one she would like. She points to a lemonade lolly that I happily buy.

As we walk along the road, I ask about the day, what she did at school. Unlike all the children I have ever known who say 'I don't know' or 'I can't remember', she lists the activities.

'I did some drawing, then some maths and played with sand.'

Her drawings do not leave a lot to the imagination, but Miss Jacobs didn't mention anything untoward in what she saw. In terms of maths, I have no idea if she is any good with numbers or not; but sand I can imagine was quite sensory, and she will have enjoyed that. With so much going on in her life and head, I am pleased that they included opportunities like this. It makes me think that perhaps they are looking at her holistically. Maybe they really will be able to meet her needs. I must ask them if they've received any information from Abby's social workers.

I am quickly taken from my thoughts: Abby is bashing at her wrist, utterly distressed. Her face is contorted into an anguished scream. What on earth has happened? It seems to be just a few drops of ice that is freaking her out. I reach into my bag and grab some tissues. I wipe her wrist where the lemonade lolly has melted down her hand and along the top of her arm.

It suddenly occurs to me that the melted lolly looks like sperm. I make sure that every last drop is gone and wrap the lolly handle with a tissue to catch the drips. I keep walking. I take her the longer route home. She won't know, and it will allow her to unwind from that real fear and trauma. And give me more time to find out if my suspicion is right.

I walk up the hill and along the top road that circles the town. I'm well aware that I am asking a leading question. 'Did,' I hesitate, not knowing quite how to phrase my question. 'Did the other one, the one you told me about, did his weenie leak on you?' (I overheard her say something to Jackson about a 'weenie' so deliberately choose this word.)

'The other one put his weenie in my bum, or he made me pull it until lemonade came out.'

Oh no. It is one of those moments when I hate to be right. Dare I push this further?

'Abby, was this one of Daddy's friends? Someone at the church?'

She shakes her head. 'No. He didn't like Daddy.'

I have a penny-drop moment.

'Did Mummy have a new boyfriend?'

Abby looks at me, right in the eyes, and nods.

'Is he the other one who did that to you?'

Another nod.

222

'He was a nasty man and he should not have done that to you. It was not your fault. Do you hear me: it was not your fault.'

I am surprisingly calm. Of all the disclosures children have made to me over the years, I know that the very last thing any of them should feel is shame. I am not an expert, but sometimes you are forced to learn a lot on the job.

I change the subject and talk about toys and favourite food and so on until we get closer to our house. And I think about Abby's adoptive mother. What bloody awful taste in men.

Before we get to the door of the house I stop and say, 'Abby, you're a good girl and you have done brilliantly at school today. Feel proud of everything you have achieved. I'm so sorry that adults have been horrible to you in the past. That's wrong. Very wrong!'

She says nothing, but this time I somehow know that she is listening.

Chapter 12

The next few days seem to be good. Bedtime is still a hard job but I reassure myself that it's still early days. Lloyd reminds me that Lily took about eight months to get into bed and sleep. She had been left in front of a glaring massive widescreen day and night. She also could not settle down if the room was quiet: she had been so used to loud and bright. I let her go to sleep to the radio in the beginning; sometimes at the weekend she would be fast asleep while booming club music blared out from the speakers. I tried her on the boys' story CDs and nursery rhymes, but she could not settle because it was not hectic enough. Now she goes to bed with a book and turns the light off when she is ready to sleep. That has taken five years, almost half her life. I don't think any of us realise just how hard it is for these children – and I don't think many people outside fostering know just how much consistent effort goes into helping change their patterns of behaviour. I have read a lot about addictions, and parallel the coming off drugs process to that of an abused child coming away from an unhealthy home culture, relinquishing their hold on the grip of negativity that was their normal.

Sometimes I wonder if foster carers realise just how much dedication is needed before they begin; how much digging for hope and strength you have to do.

I receive an email from Tortoise Tiger Lily telling me that it has been decided that Abby is to have contact with her adopted mum, Sarah.

Instantly I forward it to Lloyd and to Jane, accompanied by three question marks.

Jane gives me a call almost straight away. I tell her about Abby's latest disclosures and the delicate work going on with her right now. 'This is bound to launch her into another place once more – and I suspect a bad place. We're beginning to turn a corner here, Jane. I have noticed a soft change in her. I think she is beginning to feel – dare I say – safe? Or at least a little safer than she did.'

Jane plays devil's advocate for a moment. 'But you've talked about her affinity with her adoptive mother. She must miss her. A visit could do her good, perhaps?'

'She must miss her mum. Of course she must. But her feelings are all jumbled up. She is only six years old, and I reckon her emotional age is about three. Sometimes I wonder what planet some of these social workers are on.'

'Not this one.'

So, actually, Jane is entirely in agreement with me. I find her so refreshing – and I know that I would take her advice if she offered a different view, because I get a strong feeling that she has the child at the centre of our collective work – as do I. Sometimes this gets lost in translation, and paperwork. That other lot I can't quite figure out; maybe it is a policy to offload children who are expensive – or would be expensive if the health and education assessments found that they had to have additional support. Sometimes I am at a loss. But Jane is like us: invest in the young child rather than spend on mopping up the corporate neglect.

Lloyd comes into my studio, where I am talking to Jane on the phone, and loudly pronounces 'No' in reference to the contact visit.

'You can hear what Lloyd thinks,' I say to Jane. 'And I agree. I think it's too soon and an all-round rubbish idea.'

'Ok, here's what you do: write an email back to Tortoise Tiger Lily and outline all our concerns. Copy me in. Then she will write an email and copy us in.'

'Or Tortoise can simply ignore them.'

It gives me some small satisfaction to abbreviate her name.

And Tortoise does exactly that. Neither we nor Jane receive any further response. What I do get is an email a week later informing me that contact has been arranged outside Birmingham: a halfway point between both of us. Birmingham? *Birmingham?* That's three and a half hours away. That's an entire day given over to a bad idea.

What really riles me is that Tortoise has added a little qualifying sentence at the end of her email:

We expect you to be available as you are registered Fostering Plus.

So she's back to that again. Fostering Plus means that after so many years and training, and with all our qualification and experience, we took a grand pay rise from 30 pence an hour to 55 pence. Crack open the vintage Moet.

Oh, and we can claim petrol at 45 pence a mile. I laugh at this because it means that the car earns almost as much as us together – because that 55 pence is between the two of us.

I forward Tortoise's email to Jane and Lloyd. I know that Lloyd is literally in the studio next door, but we still treat it like work. And I sat in an office once where I emailed my colleague who sat opposite and asked her if she wanted a coffee. It makes me smile.

Lloyd and I talk about how and when to tell Abby about the meeting. We have learnt that she is not good with change or shock – even though when her feelings are heightened and scared, shock and violence are her first reaction. It is a behaviour that must have been learnt from her care-givers, or don't-care-givers.

We agree that the less time she has to think about this, the better. I am due to take her to Birmingham on the Sunday, so maybe we should tell her on Saturday. Perhaps her first reaction will be excitement and before she has too long to think about it we will be on our way. That's in a week or so.

The children gradually seem a little happier around Abby. We are creating a house where she operates in a different way, taking advice from the educational psychologist who phones up to make an appointment to see Abby. She introduces herself as Dawn and is lovely and very helpful. She suggests that I keep a separate life in the house for Abby, by giving her separate meal times and keeping her away from the other children. She also lets it slip that when she read through Abby's notes, it was clearly stated that she should not be placed with other children after one particular incident in a placement. I would love to know what that incident was, but no further information is forthcoming. I feel my blood boil again. It is so irresponsible to not be honest in this sector. We make an appointment for Dawn to come and see Abby the Tuesday after she has had the contact visit. I ask Dawn what she thinks about the contact arrangement. She isn't aware that it is happening, but expresses several concerns.

'Of course, I can't impose or enforce my views onto children's social services; all I can do is recommend – and sadly, all too often, they ignore our recommendations.'

Don't I know it. We say goodbye. Still, it feels as though things are moving. Slowly arrangements are being put into place to help Abby. I pace about a bit. It helps.

To make things work I have to plan structured time and activities around Abby specifically. When she comes home from school, we bake biscuits or do some painting. The pattern of colour covered up by darker black lines or blocks of solid black and grey repeats. I get her involved in choosing her individual food menu: she likes beans with sausages on toast followed by sliced banana and ice cream with sauce.

The week goes on. We manage a steady ship: we are usually a laid-back household and find this strict regime exhausting – and not much fun for anyone. We are not natural micro-managers. I really dislike it, and my writing and painting has taken a back seat, which is not good when I have deadlines lurking on the horizon. We literally have to know where Abby is all the time: every single second of every single hour of every single day. It still takes us an hour or so to get her to settle at night. She still gets up multiple times and I generally have to spend another half an hour settling her back into bed. Before anyone offers any ideas and techniques, I suspect that I have probably tried them all.

One evening after her bath I use Lily's sock technique and spend time drying Abby's hair with the hairdryer to make it curly. She can't leave her head alone, twirls the curls, looks in the mirror, delighted at her new image. I am reminded again of her strange behaviour with masks. This really is a child who wants to be someone else. We do her nails with some clear nail varnish. She loves all the fuss and waits patiently while I take a difficult call. A fellow foster carer rings to update me on a problem she is having. Abby can't hear the details, but she can see that I am distressed by what I am hearing from my friend and stops playing several times to give me a hug. When I get off the phone she strokes my arm and asks in a very adult-sounding way whether I am alright. It is the first time I have sensed any kind of empathy from her. I feel that we have made a tiny breakthrough if she can think about the feelings of other people. One-to-one, with my undiluted focus of attention, she is manageable.

I manage to get an appointment with Mr Brown, Abby's headteacher. He has prepared some paperwork for me in the form of lots of coloured lines. This is different from the other children's school, where they have more words in their reporting. I like the patterns, but they don't make a great deal of sense.

'Do you mind telling me what the colours mean?'

He smiles, and takes time to take me through the milestones for Key Stage One. I soon realise that Abby has not actually met *any* of them, in spite of the pretty pictures in front of me.

I feel totally deflated, and tell him so.

'Don't be. There are certainly things we can do. I'd like to have a meeting with Abby's social worker, her class teacher Miss Jacobs, and Mrs Robinson, our SENCO worker,' he explains. He doesn't need to spell out that SENCO stands for special educational needs coordinator; I've been here before.

'So what exactly do you have in mind for supporting Abby?'

He explains that the school will do its best to support Abby, but it will come down to who will pay.

I mutter something about 'virtual school'. This is a tool used by local education authorities up and down the country with the aim of supporting the education of children in care. 'But I don't currently know where we are with funding.'

'Look, Mrs Allen. We have a high number of children with different needs in this school, which could be seen as problematic on the one hand. But that *does* give our staff the experience and knowledge to deal with children whose needs are as complex as Abby's are. We will do our best, but, just as you have pointed out with 'virtual school', it does all come down to funding. Which is why we need to have the meeting.'

'Have you received the education assessment from the other county?' I ask, remembering that we are yet to see it.

'No, but the SEN team are chasing it. The email addresses given to me by Abby's social worker – whose name escapes me – have bounced back.'

I resist the temptation to supply the name 'Tortoise' for him. Instead I get out my phone and write down Annie's and Kate's names, emails, telephone numbers and office addresses.

He does a quick check with what they have on file. 'Yes, there are a couple of digits wrong. She must have made a mistake.'

I say nothing. There are far too many 'mistakes' already in this paperwork. I try not to feel any more suspicious of Tiger Lily and her cronies. I change the subject. 'So, how is Abby getting on with other children?' I ask, wondering if I really want to know the answer.

'Well, we recognise that there is some socialisation work to be done. Abby does actually seem to have taken a dislike to some children in the classroom.'

Why am I not surprised? But I like the euphemism of 'some socialisation work to be done' – I might use that myself.

'But,' he continues, 'she has made a friend. She plays nicely with one of the Portuguese children who, like Abby, seems to have a similar lower emotional age. It's early days, mind you. She hasn't really been here long enough to truly settle in. Give her time.'

After school we have an unannounced visit from Tortoise, who apparently happened to be in the area. I find that I dislike this woman more each time I encounter her. The only social workers who are formally allowed to do an unannounced visit are our supervising social workers. In practice, Lily's social worker is so lovely that we all adore her and if she turns up unannounced we welcome her like a family member and lavish her with tea and cake. But Tortoise has not got many of the personal qualities that Lily's social worker has, and I am beginning to suspect that she lacks some of the professional ones, too. I sense collusion between her manager and the other county social workers. The falsified documentation has made me deeply suspicious of all sorts of things.

Nevertheless, I politely ask Tortoise how she is, even reminding myself to call her 'Tiger Lily'. And make her a cup of herbal tea. She tells me that all the arrangements are in place for Sunday's contact with Abby's adoptive mum.

I ask her how much she knows about Abby's mum – Sarah – and what she is doing these days.

'It's quite a story,' Tortoise offers – too sensationally for my liking. 'You couldn't write it. Abby's mum left her new boyfriend Victor after they had a baby because of his anger and violence towards her and the existing children, Abby and Charlie. She had already lost contact with her husband – Charlie's dad and Abby's adoptive dad. Gordon struggled to cope with the fact that Abby was born out of wedlock and as a result of incest. He was a religious man, apparently. Tricky, that sort of thing.'

So tricky that you take it out on an innocent child, I think but do not say. But now she tells me something that I do not already know and am shocked by.

'Worse, Sarah had a trial reconciliation with the boyfriend, and is actually pregnant again. She has already decided to put this baby forward for adoption.'

Wow. It *is* some story. I feel myself sink into my chair. This woman has gone full circle: from adopting a child to having a child adopted. It is too complicated to articulate my thoughts about this woman that I know only by proxy.

'So, in your honest opinion, if this woman – Sarah – is pregnant and going to give the baby up for adoption, do you really think it's a good idea for Abby to see her?'

An unreadable expression clouds her face. For a moment I think that Tortoise might say something that she actually feels, might offer an opinion or an idea of her own. But, true to form, she responds, 'It's what my managers have decided.'

I am just about to explain that we haven't delivered the news to Abby yet because we want to carefully manage her expectations, when in rushes Abby flapping her arms around and clicking her wrists.

Before I have a chance to say anything, Tortoise high-fives Abby along with a 'hey!' for good measure. I know that I must be quite old-fashioned in this regard, but I am never comfortable with adults getting 'down' with the kids. It just makes me cringe inside. I struggled with some of my colleagues trying to be hip when I taught at the university.

But suddenly it is me who looks like the villain in this piece when Tortoise says, 'So, Abby, are you excited about seeing your mum, then?'

Chapter 13

Tortoise makes a rapid departure in the midst of the chaos that her inadvertent announcement causes, leaving me with a now re-traumatised and utterly confused little girl to deal with.

I spend the evening neglecting the other children, my husband and the dogs and cat while I try my hardest to answer Abby's questions. The biggest one of which is, 'Does Mummy love me?'

Check that in your file, Tortoise, I think – rather unkindly. Because I am at a loss. At times like this you become deeply aware of words. How, if poorly used, they can become an indelible mark on a child's mind and heart. I feel the weight of responsibility pour over me as I sit by Abby's bath while she splashes around. I can almost physically feel the whirl of thoughts, emotions and memories that must be rushing through her. Her fragile body actually contorts and contracts in a visceral way, as though all the memories are forcing their way through her veins and arteries. I watch a poor young child be reignited by all that has happened to her in the past, simply because a manager who she has never met has decided – for whatever reason – to put her back in front of the adult she invested so much love in, but who let her down. Moreover, an adult who, and I can't shift the thought, is now just about to let down another child. I know that she must have her reasons, and I know that I need to walk a mile in someone else's shoes before I judge them, but the sadness I feel is just too heavy.

As a child who also grew up navigating through the adults' mess around me, I feel that somehow, between us, we are *all* letting Abby down. She is just a child. Annoying, demanding, and challenging as she can sometimes (often?) be, she didn't ask for any of this.

Sometime after I think she has gone to sleep, I am woken from my own uneasy slumber by the sound of thumping from Abby's room. When I open the door she is in the middle of a complicated gymnastic routine involving handstands and jumps from various pieces of furniture. She leaps down to the floor and embarks upon a flurry of press-ups.

'Are you okay?'

'I want mum to love me. If I am strong I can look after her.'

What a thing for a child to say. It makes my heart hurt and my anger burn again – but not at Abby.

'You are fit and you are strong, Abby, and you have seemingly endless energy. But you do need your sleep.'

It takes another half an hour or so of coaxing, but eventually she is persuaded back in to bed. I lie awake thinking about how so many children's lives are at the mercy of people in offices who they have never met. People who cannot know anything about their inner worlds. I don't get any more sleep that night.

We have three nights left until Abby meets her mum. I will meet Sarah too. I am not looking forward to it at all. When foster carers are asked to undertake these contact visits nobody really takes on board the emotional imprint that leaves on us. I have quite strong feelings about this woman I have only heard about. We are told by the social workers that we need to be professional, but what does that mean? When you are nurturing fragile tender hearts that have Disney expectations of their families, how are you meant to behave? A child who wants to please the people who have hurt her, and we – no matter what we know – have to sit politely and quietly whilst we wait for the fallout of whatever the contact will bring.

Trauma is not something that is set in stone. It's something that is alive, on the move. It slides about, creeping into a child's being, invading their thoughts and dreams. Some days it sits quietly alongside them, but it is always following them everywhere they go. Maybe, while it keeps quiet, they can repair a little. Then other days it comes back and crashes through them, beating and stamping on all that they have within them that is good.

One of my most hated expressions used by social workers is 'Children are robust'. I suspect Tortoise's manager believes that. Given the way that she has behaved, I am sure that for now, Tortoise herself believes that. But children are *not* robust. They only have what we have given them, what they know. Their experience of time is different from an adult's: their timelines in life have not yet given them the ability and opportunity to reflect yet. They still have blind faith in us – the stupid ridiculous adults who continue to let them down.

When I looked at my own file and realised who I really was and how I was let down by the 'system', I became conscious of an overwhelming reality: a reality in which I didn't matter, because no one stepped up to help. In Abby's case, I know that she should never have been placed with us, never have been placed into a family with other children. I can see that love from the adults around her needs to go just to her, only to her, not shared amongst a crowd. She has to be the focus of all attention, everything directed at her. Given her start in life, she deserves that, and we are not the people to give it to her. I am so worried that she will not get anywhere close to knowing that she matters. Where is the person who will step up for her? While I resolve to do my best for her in the time that she remains with us, I also know that it will be nowhere near good enough. It's a horrible circle to try to square.

When I collect Abby from school it is exactly as I thought it would be: the news that she is seeing her mother has sent her into a whirling vortex, a downward spiral that unravels all the progress and settling that she has been busy doing. She has not had a good day. There had been progress of sorts, even if it isn't the sort that can be measured in Key Stage One milestones and coloured graphs and wiggly lines. But Miss Jacobs reports that Abby has been aggressive, repeatedly, and has had to do time out three times today. 'We know what she is like, but today has been really, really hard.'

I explain to Mr Brown and Miss Jacobs exactly what has gone on in the background. They are kind and understanding and promise to occupy Abby with nurture activities such as watching films and playing instruments.

'I'm afraid that it will be like this, at least until after she has seen her – and then I can't predict what will happen. It could go one of two ways. The poor child's head is all over the place and I haven't got any power to protect her. All I can do is be here.'

We discuss what can be done over the next few days. They describe various opportunities for art and expression, and her favourite activities: playing with sand and water, separately and together. It can feel absorbing and give her that important sense of mindfulness that she really needs right now. It doesn't sound like much, but at least they are on side.

I have a huge sense of failure and inadequacy as a carer. I think back on my own situation. I fought my way out of my own trauma because I realised I had choices and developed a sense of control over my own life. I have often said that the reason I think I survived my own childhood was because I ran away: I went under the radar. I came out of the system. And here I am now, as part of that very system. I feel the same sense of powerlessness as I did back then, before I made the decision to run away. As a foster carer, and as a child in care, it feels as though you have no power over your own life. There is nothing I can do for Abby to prevent this visit from happening, and I am in charge of providing the support to enable it to take place, both logistically and emotionally. Foster carers have no autonomy to advocate for the child – if you do you are soon punished, as I have found out.

I am beginning to sink into a sort of despair for this child and I feel guilty for any minute of time that I spend with my other children. It is impossible. I don't know what to do.

Back at home I feel the mood in the house fast turning into resentment. My focus has been on Abby, but I understand the unfairness of this, and now I need to think more about how this is making the other children feel.

When Lloyd and I disagree about a child, I tend to go quiet and carry on. Lloyd is furious with the way the social workers have behaved towards Abby – and us. He articulates what I do not.

'Why do fostering families feel that they are not entitled to have feelings and rights? We are not bloody robots!'

Each hour before the scheduled contact becomes more deeply engulfed in anguish, as I dance around a set of people plunged into pain because of the original act of a selfish uncle on another innocent child who we will never meet.

It's Saturday, and I struggle to find ways to pass the time with Abby while essentially ignoring my other children. Lloyd and I are working hard to keep them all separate. Jackson is out at rugby training and Abby is only out of my sight for a couple of minutes while I load the washing machine, when I hear a crash come from Jackson's room. Abby is attacking Jackson's gaming chair like a wild thing. It is his pride and joy, his most cherished thing, and by the time I make it in she has already ripped off one of the arms.

I know that Abby's mind is whirling all over the place and she has her reasons, but I love my son and I know that we will have to find the money to pay for a new one. Children's social care will not pay for the damage caused by a child. Before all the cuts they used to pay for broken windows and so on, but the reality is that they have made it so hard now to claim anything that people don't bother.

I have to check that I am not depressed. I feel hopeless. Am I depressed? Or am I suffering from working in an impossible system, one in which I have no autonomy?

I sit with Abby while she makes her mum a card. I encourage her to make flowers out of paper so we can stick them on to the front of the card. We practise writing a message for her mum on a separate piece of paper.

Mummy I love you she writes out twice, to make sure that she has it just right.

I hold back my own tears – I can almost feel physically the hope that courses through Abby's little body. Sometimes, when you have looked after a child and have become attached to them, there can be a sting for the carer as they prepare their ward to see their family: a mix of fear, concern and a hint of possessive jealousy as you watch them go to their mum or dad. With Abby, all I feel is anxiety. We are living with a girl who is probably one of the most traumatised children we have ever met, and here I am aiding or adding to that trauma by sanctioning this visit. I don't feel good about this.

We make some sponge cakes. She mixes up the butter icing and sticks it on the top of the cakes and finishes them off with jellybeans. We carefully place them into a tin ready for our early departure in the morning: it will be way before the others are up in order to meet the allotted appointment time. To help keep Abby calm, Lloyd has taken the others out to a later viewing of the latest *Star Wars* film at the cinema, and will buy them a meal on the way home. I have prepared a gentle evening with Abby to try to help her settle for the morning. In spite of her attachment to the Darth Vader outfit, she doesn't really seem to have any sense of what *Star Wars* actually is, so she doesn't make any suggestion that she might be missing out. I have really resigned myself to thinking that her penchant for that dark robe is something to do with her early experiences of religion and the priesthood.

I make her favourite dinner of chicken nuggets, chips and beans, which I allow her to smother in ketchup, and this is followed by Arctic Roll. The pudding is her choice entirely.

I didn't know it still existed outside the childhood memories of people in their fifties, but apparently it does. I nod to the plenty of strawberry sauce she adds to cover up the ice cream and sponge. She eats it all up, and even seems to make an effort with careful chewing and nicer table manners. Little steps forward like this really do feel like a giant leap.

My mobile goes: it is a dear friend of mine, Nora, who knows all about the situation, and who I know wants to wish me luck for tomorrow. I leave Abby snuggled on the sofa with some sweets while I go into the kitchen to quickly chat to my friend – because I am referring to tomorrow and to Abby's mum, I'm anxious that she doesn't overhear the conversation. Nora says all the right things and gives me just the boost I need to get through what I am considering to be something of an ordeal – for me as well as Abby – tomorrow. After a few minutes I come back in to the sitting room and Abby lifts her camouflage blanket up on one side to beckon me to share it and sit close to her, which I do. We watch the same animated film twice over because that is what she wants to do. It isn't particularly good the first time, but if she is enjoying it and settled, I'm happy with that.

Eventually I convince Abby that she needs to get to bed because we have to set off very early in the morning to see her mum near Birmingham. I show her on a map where we live and where mum is coming from and where we are meeting just outside the city. I am not sure if she fully understands the geography, or has any idea of the distances we will be covering in miles (let alone the emotional ones!), but I always try to inform the children about what we expect them just to blithely do.

It is late, just after ten o'clock, when I hear the others come through the front door with Lloyd. They all pile into the sitting room, hoovering up any sweets that are left. I ask if they have all had a good time.

'Amazing, mum!'

Vincent does impersonations of key characters and there is much discussion of how they might use 'the force'. Who needs to see the actual film? His rendition makes me feel as though I was there.

I am so pleased that they have had a good time, and that against all the odds Abby is asleep in bed. I feel that I have regained some ground, and some control. Everything is prepared for our early start: I have sorted drinks, snacks and directions. I ask the children to get their pyjamas on and promise that they can stay up for another half hour. They are all on such a high that there would be no chance of sleep in the immediate future anyway. They love that idea, and happily disappear off to their bedrooms to get changed.

Lloyd sits down next to me with a contented sigh. 'At last, some sense of normality.'

'Cheers to that,' I say, holding up my mug as though it is a victory trophy.

That sense of normality lasts for a full 10 seconds.

Until all three of the children come down – still fully dressed – but in tears, holding broken precious objects.

Abby has clearly done a swoop around the rooms, smashing anything that was loved and cherished. It is somehow much more – and much worse – than mindless violence.

'But I was with her the whole time! There is no way...' I break off, remembering my phone call.

'No wait. I took a phone call in the kitchen. From Nora. But it was only for a few minutes, and Abby was safely tucked up on the sofa when I left *and* when I came back into the sitting room. I didn't think she'd even moved from that spot. I didn't hear a thing.'

Lloyd is furious.

The children are devastated, becoming more so as they realise the true extent of the destruction. Vincent can barely get the words out through his sobs, 'She's rubbed off all my drawing from the blackboard wall – that took hours – and ripped up all my pictures of Nerf guns and planes.' For the crowning glory, he isn't able to speak at all, but merely lifts up his much-beloved toy, a small, soft Winnie the Pooh replica that has been his comforter since he was tiny. It is in two pieces: a leg has been violently ripped off, leaving stitching and stuffing on display. It seems very calculated. There is no way that Abby doesn't know how important that toy is to him. Slowly, I go upstairs to Lily's room, dreading what I might find there.

The curtains have been yanked off the rail and clothes emptied from the chest of drawers. It is as if this room has been totally ransacked. If I didn't know better I would say that we had been burgled. But those are the easy things to fix: peripheral damage. The real issue is that all the horses in her beloved cardboard stable are broken.

In Jackson's room the other arm is now off the gaming chair, and his games boxes have been ripped apart, emptied and strewn all over the floor with deep gouges scratched into the CDs.

I am certain that this is much, much more than unthinking destruction. Abby has targeted all the things that they each prize most. And she has done it ruthlessly and efficiently in a matter of a few minutes – then covered up her actions like some kind of master criminal. I don't doubt that she will deny all knowledge of what has happened.

Every door is open upstairs apart from Abby's. I peek in. She is sleeping soundly.

Something in me finally snaps and I begin to cry.

Chapter 14

Once again, I don't get much sleep.

Lloyd and I lie side by side in silence. I know that if he could, Lloyd would right now drive Abby to the offices of the children's social services and leave her there. I know that of course he won't do that, not least because he can't. Like all foster carers, we are held to ransom. If we did that, they would take Lily away: the girl who is now embedded into our family.

I feel waves of anger and sickness that wash over me the whole night through. And the question that just keeps going round and round my head: Why do we do this?

At least Abby will be away from the children for the day. We will have to think about how to make them feel better about the sabotage of their possessions. But I am so confused by Abby's behaviour – the motivation more than the cunning Houdini-like way she went about it. Going by my own mantra that all behaviour is an attempt at communication, just what the hell is she telling us?

She has been preparing to see the one person she feels that she loves. She is excited. She had my focus for the whole day, and she had her own special evening where she made all the choices about what we ate and what we watched. Why then did she want to upset the other children?

I am out of bed long before it is light. Lloyd is sleeping so I decide not to wake him. We have both lost so much sleep since Abby came into our lives. After the events of yesterday he deserves more rest.

I get Abby up. Yesterday we chose a new outfit for her to wear to see her mum, so she gets dressed quickly and quietly, with no fuss, and I make no reference to what happened last night. After we have had some breakfast – not that I feel in the slightest like eating anything – I quickly pop back upstairs to check on the other children. Jackson is asleep. He has piled up all his games as neatly as possible with their now broken cases: games that he had saved up for. A collection carefully cultivated. Both broken arms of his gaming chair are on his desk, now redundant.

Vincent is hugging Winnie very tightly. All his broken and ripped items still lie on the floor. Clearly he was in no mood to begin to right the chaos last night. I chalk up *I love you. Have a good day* on his blackboard wall.

I go in to see Lily, who has piled up all her horses and put them on a little pillow on her desk, as if to make them more comfortable in their broken distress. The cardboard stable she has attempted to tape back together.

I feel utterly, doubly devastated: so sad for them all, and so betrayed. I can really say it now: I feel that we have all, including Abby – perhaps she most of all – been betrayed and lied to and dumped on. It is all just so unfair.

It's a few minutes before 6am by the time I load Abby into the car, and not quite fully light. I double check her seat belt in the back and leave on the passenger seat a selection of snacks that I can pass backwards to her as we drive to Birmingham. I key in the postcode to my satnav and begin the drive.

Abby is quiet, I suspect still a little sleepy. I decide still to make no reference to what she did last night. I don't want to confuse or challenge her already jumbled thoughts.

I have on our usual radio station that plays jaunty music, especially at this time of day, but it quickly becomes lost as signals fade behind hills and roads. Abby asks if she can have a wee, so I pull in at a service station to take her to the loo. It's still early, not many people are about, but still I watch her hawkishly, not letting her out of my sight. I wait outside the cubicle, then check that she washes her hands. Together we queue at the coffee stand. There is one person ahead of us. Abby sings, 'I'm going to see my mummy, tralalalala' over and over, which gets us a funny look that I ignore. I grab coffee and Abby chooses a cake. As we get back into the car she seems happy.

I regularly ask if she is okay, to which I get more choruses of, 'I'm going to see my mummy, tralalalalaaa'.

In moments when she gets bored of singing, she just says the word 'mummy' to herself, over and over again, until it sounds like a siren.

The nine o'clock news comes on: it's local news and warns of slow traffic and accidents on the roads.

I call Lloyd. He is up and having his breakfast. I ask how he is and whether the children are okay.

'The children are all still asleep. It was a late – and stressful – night. I will leave them to sleep in a little longer. And I'll have a go at repairing what I can. And do you know what else I'm going to do? I'm going to tot up the cost of the damage and send it to Tortoise and to Jane.'

I laugh at how 'Tortoise' has so naturally become Tiger Lily's name now.

'Well, they won't give a hoot, we both know that; but it makes a point, I guess.'

'I have already added up Jackson's scratched CDs,' he goes on. 'They alone come to £370. Do you know that he has been collecting them for four years?'

I feel that sinking feeling – we are never going to be able to cover the replacement cost of this. But I don't want to add to Lloyd's woe. There are no solutions. We can't keep propping up children's social care.

'And they haven't refunded the cost of Abby's new school uniform yet,' Lloyd reminds me.

I feel too down to continue the conversation. The whole thing is too depressing. I don't want to keep talking about it.

'I had better go,' I tell him, and promise to call him when we get there. I wonder if social workers realise what pressure they put on people. I wonder if Tortoise has any idea what this day is doing to us all.

According to the satnav we are still 45 minutes away from our destination. I constantly check on Abby in my mirror, and point out the signs for Birmingham to give her something to look out for. As we get closer she begins to swing her legs and shake her hands until they make the customary wrist-click. She works herself up into a near-frenzy of excitement. The 'Mummy-mummy' sing-song chant gets louder and faster, like some kind of ritual incantation.

I allow myself to think some more about her adoptive mother, Sarah. In a way I can feel for her. Her life has clearly spiralled into absolute chaos, and all from a place of kindness. I remind myself that all the way through these last few weeks I sensed that she did care for Abby. There are little clues to that everywhere. But as is so often the case, the fate of the adopted child is poor: they are not blood. I know myself that as an adopted child I was at the bottom of the pile when it came to love.

I also know that it's hard to hear that. People want to believe that that will love the adopted child as much as their birth child; but I suspect a lot goes unsaid. My emotional test would be to watch a mother and father standing with their children on the edge of a cliff waiting to be saved. When the rescue services shout, 'Pass over the first child,' I think I can guess what might happen. So much is not said because we don't want to believe it.

Now Abby's mum is thinking about having her unborn baby adopted. She has two more children with her from different fathers, a succession of failed relationships – and probably little money and support.

I also wonder how this contact idea has actually come about.

Whose idea was it? Somehow, I can't imagine that it was Sarah's. She has not seen her daughter for such a long time. For months now, almost a year, Abby has been in foster care, with no contact from her adoptive mother. Sarah gave her up, formally let her go from her new family. Why would she want that reminder of what she has done? The more I think about it, the less I understand why I am driving so far to this meeting that in all likelihood isn't wanted. Sarah is pregnant and single-parenting already. She must have so much going on. What are we all doing this for? I want to yell the question out onto the air, but I wouldn't make myself heard over the 'Mummy-mummy-mummy' siren that emanates relentlessly from Abby.

I continue to check on Abby every few moments or so, to the point that it feels like I am using the rear-view mirror to check the back seat as much as the roads. When I finally say that we are 10 minutes away Abby dances in her seat and punches the air.

At the top of her voice she calls out, 'I'm seeing my mummy!' I feel her excitement and it does make me smile, in spite of the circumstances. I love watching happy children. My adoptive mother, who kept trying to send me back, used to say, 'Happy children are spoilt children.' It is a truly awful thing to think. The only way I can interpret that is as a terrible admission about her own childhood.

The chequered flag on the satnav points triumphantly to our destination end.

We arrive at a big car park. There is the bowling ally where Sarah will be waiting. I can see a McDonald's and a cinema, and, over the road, all the usual large high street stores.

Tortoise has told me that I can leave them together, that mum is not a threat and that she has talked to mum, who would like to have some time alone with Abby.

Eventually we find a parking space and get out of the car. I grab the cakes and card from the boot. I hold Abby's hand as we cross the very busy car park. She is skipping with joy. I see a number of people hanging around in the foyer and look for a lady with blonde hair. I have no other descriptive detail to go on, but no doubt Abby will recognise her.

I watch Abby to see if she can see her mother. Then I ask her directly if she can help me to find her. She looks quickly at people and dismisses them, and drags me across to corners to inspect the area to see if she is sitting down.

'She must be close by. Don't worry, we'll find her in a minute,' I tell Abby. 'We are a few minutes early, anyway.' I check the watch on my wrist, finding myself shaking it

– perhaps in unconscious imitation of Abby. We wait and walk around. I check the wall clock and my watch against the digital display on my phone.

We walk back out to the front. Finally Abby sees her and begins jumping up and down. Phew: my heart had begun to beat a little faster, as I was beginning to think she wasn't coming. But the lady walks straight by; it is not Sarah. It is not her mum.

I have been given a phone number. I give it a call: there is no answer.

I have got the out-of-hours desk number. I decide that I will give it a call if she is not here in another 10 minutes. Abby drags me around the car park to look for her. I pray that she is standing in the entrance to the bowling alley as we walk back. She is not.

I find a seat and sit down and place the cake tin and the card on my lap. I call the number. I get hold of a social worker on shift. I explain who we are and where we are and what we are doing. I ask if they have any information. The social worker asks me to wait while they make some calls. I try to smile reassuringly at Abby, but she looks worried: the smile has dropped completely from her face. I pull her into me and try to cuddle her, but she begins to flap.

I watch people stare at her. I can feel her anxiety.

After 15 minutes, the social worker calls back and says that he has tried mum's number but there is no answer.

I explain again, as patiently as I possibly can, that I have already been doing this. I remind him that she is in the latter stages of pregnancy. 'Perhaps something has happened?'

'I don't know, and I don't really know what else you can do. Perhaps wait for another half an hour, then think of returning home?' I know that he is trying to be helpful, but we are no further forward.

Abby is shaking her hands so much that I am concerned that she may hurt herself. I stroke down her hand and say 'Shhh,' in the most soothing voice I can muster. Meanwhile I keep calling Sarah's number – as does the man on the out-of-hours desk.

I call Lloyd.

'How it's going?' he asks, brightly.

I explain what's happening.

He swears.

'I will get us some lunch, then come back. Not sure what else we can do, really.'

Lloyd begins ranting down the phone about the waste of time, money and resources – and what about Abby's feelings?

Abby's feelings are becoming increasingly apparent – to everyone in the vicinity. She is, by now, sobbing hysterically. I ignore everyone else and sit her on my lap. I resist her pulling away until eventually she leans right in and cries and cries and cries.

I wait for a long time until the sobs subside, until it feels okay to wander over to get a burger. I hope that Abby is able to eat something, and I am pretty peckish. I had never eaten in a 'family fast food restaurant' until I had my own children, and since we began fostering I must confess that they have become quite familiar.

By half past three in the afternoon I have fed Abby, walked her round, bought her treats and toys, and put her, howling, back into the car. There is nothing more for us here. And nothing can console her after what she surely must perceive as another rejection in the long list of them in her life. I double check her belt and hope that she sleeps on the way home. I tap 'Home' into the satnav and quickly call Lloyd. It goes straight to answerphone, so I just leave a quick message. 'No luck. We are leaving now. Mission aborted. See you all soon. Love you.'

Chapter 15

We drive home, through red traffic light after red traffic light, it seems. This first part of the journey is jerky and stop-start. The city traffic is dense. Another hour has passed and we don't seem to have got very far at all. It's already 4pm and we still have many miles to go. Abby is staring out of the window clutching the Darth Vader toy I just bought her. I feel so sad for her. I wish Sarah, her mum, had at least told us that she couldn't make it. Or even just spoken to Abby on the phone. I have no idea what is going on, only that I have an already broken child in a few more bits strapped into the car. Because we don't know exactly what's happened I can't relax into being cross: what if it was something to do with the pregnancy? That would be some sort of explanation for her no-show. But it's not really a conversation I can have with Abby, who doesn't need reasons right now – she just needs not to be rejected in the way that she has been – and I can't sort that out.

I keep driving. The radio crackles in and out of tune from time to time. I keep driving. I check on Abby, who has finally cried herself to sleep. In the rear-view mirror I can see the little rivers of dried tears sticky across her cheeks. I keep driving. At least we are beyond the city and the traffic flow is better now. We can actually pick up some speed and put some distance between us and that scene of disaster. I keep driving. Somehow we eat up the miles. The names on the road signs become more familiar as we get nearer to areas that I know well. The sun begins to go down on a difficult day. I keep driving. It gets darker. White lines light up the side of the road. It becomes difficult to concentrate – a combination of the monotony and my own tiredness. I keep driving.

I can hear the little sniffly sleep noises from Abby, the shuddering aftermath of the sobbing that rises within her periodically disturbing the peace of slumber. I keep driving. The radio finally kicks back in to a channel that I know. I start to hum along to some tunes. At this time of day they are more introspective than this morning's jangly offerings.

Shit!

Oh shit!

From nowhere, Abby has undone her belt and has her hands across my face. I can't see anything. I shout at her to get off me. I slow down from hurtling along in the middle lane, where I have just overtaken someone, but there is traffic all around me and I can't pull over. I don't have time to consciously make that decision, though. Because now she climbs over into the front seat and begins hitting me. It hurts. There is a surge of power within her. All the anger and frustration she feels at being let down is being taken out on me. She screams at the top of her voice, 'I hate you! I hate you!' All the time she pounds her little fists into me and lashes out. This all happens so quickly. It is only a few seconds from her holding my eyes to being next to me in the front.

I lose control of the car completely, swerving across another lane to the right.

We veer off into a crash barrier. The airbag shoots into action and I am flung back into my seat. At the same time Abby is thrown into the back.

I think I lose consciousness for a moment. Then when I come to, it takes a few minutes for me to understand what has just happened. There are people standing at the passenger window, peering in. One is calling out, 'Are you alright?'

I nod. I think so, bewildered as I am. But Abby? What about Abby?

'Abby, are you okay?' I shout into the back of the car.

She is lying on the back seat, clutching the Darth Vader with her thumb in her mouth. People open both doors and check that we are okay – other motorists who have stopped as they witnessed the accident. There is a great deal of concern; they have called an ambulance. I am not to worry, everything is going to be all right. The next thing I know I am on the outside of the car, looking in. Everything is not all right. The car is damaged badly: the whole right front side is crumpled. But at least the crash barrier prevented us from driving into oncoming traffic. Bad as things are, I have a terrible vision of what might have happened.

I am still in shock. There are people everywhere around us. Flashing lights now, and actual sirens. I am astonished at the chaos we have caused. From somewhere I have a blanket wrapped around me, and am standing by the side of the road. There is a police car and an ambulance. Everything takes on an air of unreality. We are in the back of the ambulance now, though I don't remember climbing in here. I think I am still in a bit of a daze. I am talking to the paramedics and the police. I explain what happened as carefully and as accurately as I can: that Abby undid her seat belt and started hitting me. I tell them about the whole situation: where we had been today and why. About her mum not turning up at contact. The policeman asks if I want to call Lloyd. I do. I absolutely do.

Lloyd is deeply upset – and angry. He is very angry indeed; perhaps angrier than I have ever known him.

'I'm so sorry about the car,' I say. It is his pride and joy. I think it is a write-off. It doesn't look repairable, to the untrained eye at least.

'The car is not the thing that matters here!'

He is arranging a babysitter, he tells me, and will get to me as soon as he possibly can to bring us home. I tell him that we both seem fine, but that they are insisting that we go to the hospital to be checked over. 'Just as a precaution.'

'Good. Now, can you pass me over so that I can speak to a police officer who is with you?'

I think he wants the details of exactly where the car is and which hospital we are going to. He knows he isn't getting a lot of sense from me.

I sit with Abby in hospital. We are both fine, thankfully, and the hospital staff have been amazing – so reassuring and thorough. The police explain that they are writing up a report which will be sent to both sets of authorities, and impress upon me not to worry. I cannot get my head around just how we have ended up here. I don't mean that I am still confused by the accident. I mean the whole chain of events that have brought us here on this night. Whichever way I look at it, it seems as though all these events were designed by others: this accident is the result of everyone else's decisions. I feel as though I am standing still on a moving treadmill – that all this stuff has been going on around me and I have just been rolled along with it – and nearly rolled under it.

'What if' questions tumble around my head without their seatbelts on. What if we had been more seriously injured? What if we had died? What if my children lost their mother because I was looking after somebody else's traumatised child? It's all just too much to think about for my spinning head. I notice that my thoughts are all about me, and my family, and our potential losses. I didn't think, 'What if Abby had died?'

Lloyd soon arrives in the hospital and I fall into his arms. He is so happy to see me, but not nearly as happy as I am to see him. He roots me back into the real world away from this dream-like few hours in the aftermath of the accident.

Abby is sitting down quietly next to me. She has said very little. Lloyd explains that he has spoken at length to the police and that they have decided to drive back with us. One of them will sit in the back of the car with Abby to make sure she doesn't undo her belt again. I am overwhelmed once again by the idea of the enormous amount of chaos caused by that uncle nearly seven years ago. I am struck by the idea that if Abby isn't properly supported now, that chaos will continue to spiral from her hurt and trauma.

Thoughts like this cloud the rest of my journey home.

As soon as I am through the front door, I hug the children so closely. They are all crying and fussing and touching me as if to confirm that I really am there in front of them.

'If you really want to make a fuss of me you can let me sit down,' I say, and am instantly ushered to a seat. I am keen to know how they are, too, and to talk about how we will replace all their items. But they are not interested in that: Lily has sewn Winnie's leg back on for Vincent; Jackson says that he quite likes sitting in an open chair for gaming, it gives him more room to manoeuvre. 'It should be a design feature of a gaming chair, Mum.'

Lily says that maybe she is getting too old for the horses.

I love them so much it actually does hurt.

I look at Abby. She is silent, sitting in the big wingback chair, trying as always to make sense of the mad world around her. I have somehow managed to forget that we still have police here in the house, until an officer comes in to the

262

sitting room and hands me a hot drink. I can hear that Lloyd is busy bustling about in the kitchen, in my role of making sure that everyone is catered for.

'We'll be on our way, then, Mrs Allen,' he says. I follow him to the front door. He and his colleague shake our hands and we both thank them very much. The older one turns back as he steps across the threshold. 'This is off the record and anyway, I am retiring soon. I just want you to know that I have seen so much over the years, and if I were you I would think about giving notice on Abby. In my opinion, this is only going to get worse. She needs something else. You have a lovely family and you need to look after them.' He nods his head in the direction of the sitting room and says goodbye.

'He's right,' says Lloyd, after the front door is closed behind them.

And I know it. My feelings are all over the place. I have been entirely overtaken by events, but actually, the car accident has put one thing in sharp perspective: it has made me realise how important my family is. If I was standing on the edge of that cliff and the rescue services shouted out, 'Pass over the first child,' then I think I would send Abby first – because I want to inhale all the love in my family undiluted. I feel like I never want to be apart from any of them ever again.

Chapter 16

The next day we decide to send Abby to school in spite of the accident. Since she isn't injured physically, it seems the most sensible thing to do. In fact, all the children go to school. I speak at length to Mr Brown and tell him that we have no choice but to hand in notice on Abby. If it means that children's social services black-list us, then so be it. I know what's important now: we have to protect our family.

Mr Brown is as wonderfully reassuring as he has been all along. 'Over the years we had been involved with so many children and their families. We can each only do what we can.' He allows a short pause before he follows that with, 'And in your case, that is an awful lot more than most.'

He pauses again to allow that to sink in before explaining that he will put Abby in the nurture room, 'with one-to-one care'.

When I return home from the school there is no question about what I do next. Lloyd sits next to me at my laptop as I begin to type:

It is with regret that we have to give notice on Abimbola's placement. We feel that we can no longer keep her – or ourselves – safe. Due to a series of events resulting in a serious car accident we have decided to end the placement. We understand that normally we have to wait 28 days for the child to be removed but would appreciate in these circumstances if you could look at removing Abby sooner. Please see attached log of events. You will also have received an incident report from the police.

We look forward to hearing from you.
Lloyd and Louise Allen

And it is done. The relief we feel from sending that email is incredible. We sit next to each other for a few moments more, in silence, while we let it sink in. I don't even think (too much) about what the notes for this 'failed placement' might say. Actually, I hope that whoever cares for her next hears all about it. Wherever Abby goes to, she should arrive from a position of honesty and forthrightness: truth about her past and what has brought her to this point.

I break the silence and aim to strike a note of normality. 'Coffee?' I ask, breezily. I make the drinks and sit down with my mobile to call Jane.

She answers immediately. 'Louise, are you okay?' Somehow news has already reached her.

Yes, I'm fine. We are both fine. Abby was well enough to go to school today, so I have sent her in.'

And I'm telling the truth. I do feel fine. It is a huge surge that I feel from the change in power. When you have nothing left to lose (and in our case we nearly lost our lives), you don't feel like messing about. I feel assertive and back in control. I recount the entire episode to Jane, who sighs and sighs as I go over the details.

'And no word as yet about why Sarah never showed up?'

'Nothing.'

'What a bloody nightmare!'

I can feel the genuine concern in her words, and a frustration that matches my own.

'Listen, Louise, would you mind if I popped over later? I feel like I need to see you in person.'

'Of course. We're here. We'd love to see you.'

Before she hangs up she tells me that she and her managers are driving over to Tiger Lily's office in a few minutes' time. 'You know that you have our full support. I totally have your back on this.'

'Thank you,' I say, even though I tell myself that I am no longer concerned about what social services think of our care.

I go around the house picking up items for washing. I am not as fine as I think I am, because in Abby's room I suddenly burst into tears again. We are rejecting her, just as the other adults in her life have. This is another rejection on her way to becoming a self-fulfilling prophecy.

I sit on her bed and weep again, surprised to find that there are any tears left. Lloyd comes to the door and I see that his eyes are wet, too. He feels just as at sea as I do. None of this is easy. That feeling of being back in control has swiftly vanished on entering Abby's room. I know that I can't be responsible for Abby's future, and I know that I have to put the safety of my own family first, but I also know that I am condemning Abby to a troubled future in care. The terrible trajectory of her life so far is only going to get worse as she is moved from pillar to post by a system that can't cope with her needs. The best she can hope for is to be placed in some specialist therapeutic unit. She needs it – but that is expensive, and for that reason can only ever be a last resort when all else has failed.

I survey the meagre contents around the room. This is all she has, but I will not let her leave with her possessions in a bin bag. We will do everything in our power to give her dignity and respect, because Abby matters.

I am not ready to work; I still can't concentrate. I pop to the shops to buy some ingredients for dinner. I drift aimlessly about the aisles thinking morbidly about what could be happening today if I had died. How would my children be? I begin to cry again. This is a futile train of thought, but I can't help myself. I buy the children puddings and biscuits. Treats galore. Today we are all happy. We are where we are and it's okay. And I want to talk to Lloyd about perhaps keeping Abby here until there is a good new placement that we can help her transition to. I want to do right by her. It really isn't fair to turn her out, whatever has happened.

Back at home, Jane knocks at the door with her managers, a man and a woman who I have never met before. I must admit that I am not a big fan of a gaggle of social workers in my home, but collectively they are lovely and explain that they just wanted to see if I was okay and to ask if there was anything they could do. They stay for a coffee while I talk about Abby's future and my wish to help her transition to a good placement.

Lloyd, who is not in a good mood with children's social care right now, is cutting. 'Louise, you and I both know that will not happen.'

I swallow. The managers tell me that they must get back to the office.

'But I'll stay for a bit longer, if that's alright with you,' Jane says.

Once they are gone I tell Jane exactly how angry I feel about what has happened, how we have been duped, and how frustrated I am. It all comes out in one big incoherent jumble, because that is how it all feels in my head. Tears begin pouring from my eyes again. I honestly don't know what has happened to me. I don't usually cry like this. Lloyd puts his hand on my shoulder. He, like me, is also uncharacteristically tearful. It has all just been too much strain on us.

On all of us.

Because, albeit unwittingly, we are contributing to the cycle of rejection and the tragedy of Abby's life story.

Chapter 17

Although I am no longer a part of Abby's story, I make Jane promise to keep me in the loop with what is going on.

I was right to be worried.

Abby experiences nine more placements in the space of a year. Nine *more* placements? It's unthinkable. That's not much more than one a month. And I know from Jane that she doesn't last that long at most of them. Jane is surprisingly knowledgeable about Abby's ongoing sagas, even when Abby is moved over the border into the next county. I wonder if each set of foster carers is as unsuspecting, unprepared and unsupported as we were. Her behaviour deteriorates a little further each time. And of course, although she is small, she is capable of causing a great deal of hurt – as we already know to our cost.

She celebrates her seventh birthday in a care home. I almost want Jane to stop giving me these updates. They are so painful to hear. Has she really come round, just to tell me this?

'Not exactly. There's another reason why I am here,' says Jane. I look at her with renewed curiosity as she clears her throat and prepares to continue. Clearly some sort of announcement is coming.

'I am retiring soon.'

Oh, bloody hell. Not again. She has been our supervising social worker for a year, and I really like her. Why do all the good ones go? It isn't fair.

I reach for Lloyd's reassuring hand as she shares her news.

'I hadn't told you before, because I wanted to line up all the ducks, so to speak.'

Lining up ducks? What is she talking about? One social worker left into floristry, is she going to start some sort of smallholding?

Lloyd interrupts her and cuts to the chase. 'When are you leaving?'

'In a month. But wait, don't misunderstand me. There is more to my decision, and I wanted you to be among the first to hear. It's with very good reason.'

I don't doubt it. But it's terrible news for us.

'Don't be sad, Louise. It really is for a very good reason. I needed to make sure that everything was in place, that we were really sure that we could do it.'

Her eyes are shining – I have no idea what it is that she wants to do. Bungee jump? Sky dive? Cruise around the Med?

'My partner – Penny – and I, we're going to adopt Abby.'

That really shuts us both up. This is absolutely not what I was expecting to hear. Nor Lloyd, judging by the shocked expression on his face.

'I haven't really talked very much about her, but Penny is a great psychotherapist,' Jane goes on. 'Her specialism is sexually abused children. She has worked in this sector for over 40 years, in fact. And we both want to support Abby. We've been investigating the possibility for some time now. We are both retiring at the same time so that we can make it work.'

I jump up and give Jane a huge hug. I can't stop crying, just as when Abby first left us, but this time it is because I am so happy, so relieved.

Lloyd too gives Jane a hug, and now Jane begins to cry. We all sit down laughing and crying and not quite believing what's happening. It is a lot to take in. A marvellous lot to take in.

Jane goes on to say that she has been working behind the scenes with Penny and the adoption team to begin the assessment process. 'Even we have to go through the process – and trust me, it's a far better system here than it was for Abby seven years ago when she was first adopted.

'I was as upset as you were with the repeated failure of everyone to do for that child what she really needs. Penny and I have been meeting Abby and have already begun the process of really getting to know her.

'I didn't want to tell you before, but we have been taking her out – for short trips initially – and then last week we had her at home for the first sleepover. We have tried not to rush things – though believe me, at times I have wanted to – so that we can truly start to build the foundations of trust. We are doing everything we can to smooth what we hope will be her last transition in the care system.'

Although I am going to miss Jane so much, Abby's need is far, far greater than mine. The relief I feel is immeasurable.

'Penny and I have used all our powers to obtain all of Abby's records. We know now that Abby was removed at speed from the foster placement before yours because she attacked a child with a knife. We think that was maybe why she was sent across the country and why her records are so erratic. She has been involved in a few high-level incidents since, too, but again, I haven't wanted to tell you it all.'

I think back to that short time that Abby was with us, and the damage, havoc and heartbreak she wreaked. My children were in more danger than I ever imagined. A few broken toys feel like a small price to have paid.

'Penny has a plan, and we will both work with her day and night to help Abby feel safe. Abby is not a bad child. I watched her with you, and saw how you reached her, Louise. You and your family did so much good – and you need to know this. I know it probably doesn't feel like it.'

She pauses here for a moment, allowing those words to resonate in the air. I need to hear them.

'Abby needs years of therapy and one-to-one – well, two-to-one – to undo some of that abuse and neglect. Frankly, if we do not do this, Abby will grow up to be a threat to society, dangerous to herself and to others. She cannot regulate her behaviour. You saw that. She does not know who she is and her sense of loss is off the scale. But Penny has the experience and knowledge to help her, and I hope that I have the patience. The system didn't need too much persuading – adoption is, after all, much cheaper than foster care, and if anyone knows what they are getting into, it's me.'

Everything Jane says is everything we want, and *need*, to hear. This is the mood and the level of care I wish for every child who finds themselves in this sector.

Epilogue

It is easy to forget to just be happy on the ordinary days. Today is both an ordinary day and an extraordinary one. The timer goes to let me know that the sponge is ready to come out of the oven.

Abby was 10 years old a few weeks ago, so her birthday has already passed. She celebrated it with a trip to the cinema – to see a *Star Wars* film, I believe. It seems incredible that she is old enough to do that already. I have made a cake anyway. I don't ever need much of an excuse for cake. I suppose I am baking the cake that I thought I might bake for her when she first came to us all those years ago.

I turn the sponge out onto the cooling rack and fan the air above it with my hand, as though that is going to speed up the process. I don't have long to ice this before they will all be here.

The boys have chosen to be present of their own accord, except that I expect them to disappear off as soon as they have met Abby and said hello. But they wanted to be here. They are curious to see how she is getting on. We all are. In spite of, or perhaps because of, the difficulties that she caused us all.

I put the finishing touches to the 'storm trooper' face – very simple, with some white fondant icing and a black icing pen – just as the doorbell goes.

Abby comes rushing in, laughing and giggling and tumbling through the hallway with Penny and Jane following just behind. This time it is me who manages to save the umbrella stand as she comes crashing past, arms waving in the air, before I have a chance to invite her in. Penny and Jane have been Abby's adoptive parents for nearly three years. In that time she has clearly lost none of her energy and exuberance, but I haven't heard a wrist-click yet.

'Yes, we've been trying to encourage her to do that thing with her wrists less. I think it's working,' Jane winks at me, reading my mind – she remembers how bothered I was by it.

Abby is sporting a *Star Wars* t-shirt. Jane told me on the telephone that she no longer feels the need to wear a costume or a mask to hide, but she has an obsession with the films now that she can understand them. Developmentally, she still remains a long, long way behind her peers. Perhaps now she behaves like a six-year-old might – the sort of behaviour we were probably expecting when she arrived with us a few years ago. She is still tiny, though. She makes a big fuss of the dogs, and they of her, and soon she is outside in the garden, running round with them.

'I'll watch her,' says Penny, leaving Jane and me to chat. We haven't seen each other much in the intervening time since she retired, but we have remained firm friends and she has kept me up to date with regular information about Abby's progress. Now she tells me that she wants to fill in some of the blanks. There probably aren't that many people who will really understand the context that she has come from.

'You already knew – or guessed – about what she calls "Gordon's secret", I think; Gordon was her adoptive father, and he would regularly beat Abby in order to punish and 'purify' her from the sins of the birth mother. You were right about the marks on her body. She still has plenty of physical scars – not to mention the emotional ones. The 'purification' went on for a while. From some of the language she has used to describe Gordon's punishments, it really rather sounds as if he tried some kind of bizarre exorcism on her. It certainly sounds as if he couldn't cope with the circumstances of Abby's birth once he discovered them, and he took his disgust out on her. But in some ways he was smart, because then he would force her to swear on the Holy Bible that she wouldn't tell anyone. And because she was trying so hard in that family to be good, and to be as loved as her little brother, she obeyed him.'

'She called herself the spawn of Satan when she first came to us,' I say and shudder at the memory of it. 'Oh yes, and she hit a vicar!' I half-smile at that recollection, though it was very unpleasant and disturbing at the time.

Knowing what I now know, I'm surprised she didn't try to hurt him more.

Jane continues, 'But I think you also know that the physical abuse, in many ways, wasn't the worst of it: you were the one who put us onto that. There was neglect, that we knew about, of course. Because of the new baby, she rather got pushed to one side. The new boyfriend was a man called Victor who eventually became Sarah's second husband. We believe now that he was sexually abusing Abby, too. You had pretty firm evidence of that, I know. Penny has found out more as Abby has gone through therapy. Imagine that, the first two influential men you encounter in your life do *that* to you.'

'Can't they get him for that?'

'Nope, not a thing we can do about it. It would be the word of a young child against his. We can't prosecute without dredging things up for Abby, and that would just be too damaging. Any anyway, the defence would pull apart the testimony of a three-year-old as she was then. She couldn't possibly be a sound witness, even if we were to let her – which we wouldn't.'

'So he gets away with it. What a mess.' And what rubbish taste in men Sarah must have had, I think again. Perhaps I had a lucky escape not meeting her, that afternoon in a Birmingham car park.

'She kept the brother Charles, but put the youngest baby up for adoption. What a mess. Victor, the second husband, had left her by then, so she was a single parent again.'

I am grateful to Jane for filling in all the missing details. She has the same interest in people as I do, the same kind of need to know.

'Did you ever find out why the mother, Sarah, never showed up in Birmingham that day? The day of the accident?'

'I did follow that up. Victor stopped her from going. Probably worried that he would be found out – that Abby might tell Sarah what had been going on. I think Sarah probably would have come. I like to think so.'

'Do you think that the therapy is working?'

'I don't know. But again, I like to think so. Penny has been doing some sterling work getting Abby to begin to come to terms with it. If you ever can come to terms with something like that. I like to think of it as helping her to find a way to coexist with her wounds.'

Abby hurtles in at that moment. 'Can I have some squash, please, Wendy?'

I bridle at the use of the name, once more. Such a simple thing to get someone's name right. Or perhaps not. Jane must notice my reaction.

'Ah, yes. I found out about Wendy,' Jane explains once Abby is back outside. 'It's rather nice, actually. I think you'll like it. Abby called you Wendy because it was the name of her first foster carer. The first place that she went to after leaving Sarah and Victor. She was happy there, apparently, and after several traumatic moves she just got confused. She hoped that all foster carers would be Wendy. She never learnt anyone else's name, apart from yours. It was part of her global delay and FAS. So, in a strange kind of way, calling you Wendy was a compliment. She uses it now for anyone that she really likes. You should be honoured!' Jane gives a little laugh.

And I thought it was another way of winding me up. 'I'll take that, then,' I say.

'In many ways, it's a miracle that she is as well adjusted as she is – though of course she still has a long, long way to go, and developmentally she won't catch up with her peers. She's starting secondary school in September, but we don't expect that she will ever take any GCSEs.'

Who gives a stuff about qualifications when you weigh them up against quality of life? I think. Abby is in the best place that she could possibly be, I'm sure of it. If only every child in care had the same opportunity – but then we'd be living in some kind of utopian dream.

'And she is quite taken these days with using her full name,' Jane goes on, her thoughts evidently travelling in a different direction from mine. 'The first step in reclaiming her identity is in reclaiming her name. It's the one concrete thing that she got from her birth mother, though we'll never quite know why, but it's still something to hang on to. We have done a bit of research with her. For Yoruba tribes, Abimbola means "wealth".'

'Oh yes, I remember looking that up at the time.' I confess to Jane about the search for yams in Waitrose, and all the other ridiculous preparations I made for the arrival of what I was hoping would be a little African girl in our house.

She laughs. 'I'm sure that I would probably have done the same thing.'

'And I also know that when I found out what her name meant, I remember thinking what an irony it was for such a love-poor, rejected child.'

'True. But, do you know what? We are determined to make her wealthy in *our* love. I know it sounds a bit corny, but that's our mission. I also found out that it can mean 'honour'. You know that there was little honour to speak of in Abimbola's arrival in the world. But we're doing our best to put that right in her life now.'

We call Abby – Abimbola – and Penny back in, and Lloyd joins us for the singing and the cutting of the cake, bringing his camera with him. I have no doubt that Penny and Jane have been good at helping Abimbola to collect some happy memories this year, but I won't forget that strange photograph that was one of the few things she arrived with, and what it told me about how little she had been valued.

I have put 10 candles into the icing – even though this is a belated celebration. Still, you can never have enough birthday cake, in my opinion. We stand and sing birthday wishes to her, and when it gets to the 'happy birthday dear Abimbola' line we emphasise all four syllables of her name. Abimbola smiles round at all of us and blows the candles out in one breath with a pleased giggle. Lloyd captures the moment and promises to send on the photograph.

I hesitate, momentarily, before handing the knife to Abimbola, but do so after a little reassuring nod from Jane. Penny stands behind and helps her to cut through the storm-trooper mask. We have a slice of cake each and there is silence for a moment as we all eat. I did a good job on that sponge, if I say so myself.

I can finally feel thankful for the adults who have intervened in her life. All of us. Even though it took us a long time to get her the care and support she really needed. Look at where we are today. It truly is a world away from the trauma of the night of the accident, and the night of destruction. Those two moments are etched into our family folklore.

But, when all the cake is gone and everyone has gone home, I can't help myself from having a quick check upstairs to make sure that the rooms are undisturbed and the children's possessions intact.

They are all there, of course.

Honour is being restored.

Acknowledgements

Thank you to my beautiful blended family for all your joy, challenges and inspiration, Lloyd, Jackson, Vincent, Taryn and Chloe, Millie, Mitchell and Poppy and to all the children and teenagers I meet in my work both as a foster carer and artist. To Kate, my great friend and walker of dogs. Thank you to Mirror Books for your faith in me, to Theresa Gooda, my very clever and talented ally, and to Jo Sollis, the nicest editor one could ever hope for. Thank you to Jane Graham-Maw, my agent and supporter.

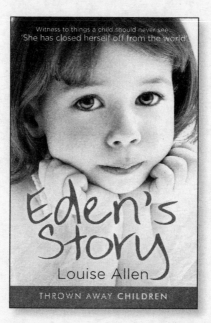

Eden's Story

Next in the Thrown Away Children series

By Louise Allen

Preview:

Chapter One

Ashley swings on the back two legs of the kitchen chair and scrolls idly through memes and images on her phone's feed, 'liking' the odd post here and there.

She sees that she is invited to follow a new florist that has been opened by a friend of a friend. Fair enough. It seems brave going into business by yourself; good on her. A nightclub has opened up on the Brampton Road where the old Octopussy used to be; a bunch of her old crowd are heading there tonight. Priscilla has updated her status to 'in a relationship'. Alright for some.

Looking great, hun, she comments beneath an image of an old school friend that she hasn't seen now for a couple of years, who has posted her freshly and perfectly manicured acrylics in close-up. They do look good, actually. Ashley clenches her own fists shut in order to avoid witnessing her chewed nails and split cuticles.

She glances absently down from her seventh floor window to the little ant people below, scurrying around down there, getting on with their business. She wonders how people have so much urgency in them. They all look so very busy, all on their way somewhere. She feels nothing but lethargy.

Sometimes seven floors feels just too high up to even bother to leave the flat and take Eden to the park for some fresh air.

Right now, Eden is fast asleep, enjoying her mid-morning nap in the next room. Ashley has about another twenty minutes or so of this guilt-free part of the day until Eden wakes. She tries to put the phone away for as much time as she can when Eden is up and about. She knows she shouldn't really be looking at a screen in front of Eden; her daughter should have her undivided attention. But then, on the other hand, what does a one-year-old know or care, really?

More scrolling and swiping. Another friend, Dana, has made a batch of fairy cakes, all beautifully frosted with elaborate decorations. Perhaps Ashley should try some baking for a change. She used to enjoy it. It's been a long time since she's seen Dana, too, Ashley thinks. She has kind of lost touch with most of the old faces. Having a baby isolates you.

The phone pings an alert, distracting her from that train of thought. It is from Christina, with her daily psychic update and advice.

Don't be too critical of yourself, Ashley. I know from our psychic reading last month that you have an awful lot of unused potential which you have not taken advantage of.

Try something new today. A flower will become significant. Sometimes your introverted nature means that people see you as wary and reserved. Try to relax so that you are more sociable.

Chance would be a bloody fine thing, Ashley thinks. There's no one to be sociable *with*. But Christina is right. She always hits the nail on the head. It's amazing how much these psychics can tell about you from just a few details. Ashley does have a tendency to be too wary – of people, of going out, of trying new things. Perhaps she *should* live a little. It's the twenty-first century. Having a baby doesn't have to mean the end of your social life. She should make the effort to get out more. Relax, like Christina says. It isn't healthy to be cooped up here all the time with a kid in such a tiny space. She is on the waiting list to move; a one-bedroom flat won't be ideal once Eden is toddling around, but it's been fine just the two of them, for now. In some ways it makes it easier to keep an eye on Eden. She's always in view, always safe. It's just being stuck up here doesn't help with meeting people and being part of a community. Ashley remembers, with a rueful smile, how she used to think it would be so much fun to live in a tower block: all those people so close together – how sociable it would be. The reality is somewhat different. Ashley has never felt as lonely as during this last year.

She moves to the sink and rinses out her coffee cup, leaving it to drain on the side. In a fit of determination she adds flour and eggs to the wipe-clean shopping list attached to the front of the fridge. Fairy cakes are straightforward. It's been an age since she last made them, and most importantly, Eden will like them. Next she forces herself to sort through the laundry basket and put another load of washing on: mostly Eden's babygros, cot-sheets and muslins. Ashley finds that she hardly seems to have any clothes any more. Nothing new, anyway. She feeds the cactus plant that is looking a little sorry for itself on the window ledge; checks her phone again. 'Thanks hun, catch up soon,' the school friend with the nice nails has replied. *Put the bloody phone down*, Ashley tells herself. Nobody's interested in you. She hears the thud of the mail falling through the letterbox onto the mat and heads into the tiny hallway to retrieve it. Something from the council. A postcard from Tessa in Lanzarote. That's nice. She didn't think anyone sent postcards anymore. An offer on pizza delivery. A copy of the local free newspaper, from which a load of junk mail immediately spills. A flyer for that new night club, the White Orchid – announcing free entry for one night only and a promotional deal on drinks.

There is a flash of yellow across the front of the newspaper, announcing in-depth horoscopes on page eighteen. *Find out what today holds in store – and how your life is going to change over the next few weeks.* Ashley sighs. Eden won't wake for a few more minutes. Time to take a look. Ashley thumbs through the pages. She scans the page and finds 'Aries' quickly.

Change is on the horizon. The world is about to turn upside down. But it is up to you to make it happen. Right now your destiny is in your hands. You will soon meet someone special, but it will take you out of your comfort zone to get there. The effort is worthwhile. Go for it!

Why not? Ashley reaches for her phone and sends a quick message to Kerry, her one remaining good friend who didn't desert her shortly after Eden was born - who has helped her out in the past and might just babysit if she isn't busy tonight.

The reply comes back within a minute.

'4 U, Ash? Course! Going somewhere special?'

Ashley reaches for the nightclub flyer and takes a quick snapshot to send back in answer. Her mind is made up. Now, what to wear? And what to do with her hair?

That's Eden stirring now. Time to be back on duty. But there is a new spring in Ashley's step, a little more energy as she heads towards the bedroom. Today is the start of something new, something big. She can feel it.

'Come here, darling! Give Mummy a cuddle. Did Eden have a nice nap? Let's get you out of there, shall we..?'

The usually long afternoon goes by in a flash. Ashley manages to paint her nails, wash and blow dry her hair and dig out a pair of stretchy black jeans that look surprisingly good – now that she has regained most of her figure – paired with black ankle boots that she forgot she had. A couple of episodes of *Peppa Pig* help keep Eden occupied while Ashley gives herself a mini-makeover. She seems to like them on repeat. Ashley tags herself into the group going to the night-club, and is pleased with the comments from old friends that sound genuinely happy that she is coming along.

'You look brilliant, Ashley!' Kerry says, out of breath, when she arrives early evening.

'Thank you!' Ashley is pleased at the compliment. She has enjoyed getting ready for this rare night out. She notices Kerry's panting. 'Are you ok? Did you walk up? Is the lift not working?'

'No, it's fine – just thought it would be a good way to get my steps up today – but the novelty wore off after the third floor!'

They giggle together.

'Almost wish I was going with you, though. You really do look terrific!'

'You know you're the only one I could trust with Eden. We'll have a good night in together soon, though, instead. Proper catch up. How's that? And a drink together now. It will give me a bit of Dutch courage; a little bit of confidence to start the night.'

'Confidence? They'll be falling at your feet. Look at you!'

Ashley explains Eden's routine carefully as they share a bottle of wine. 'But she's ever so good with sleep these days. She's been going right through for a couple of months now. You shouldn't hear a peep out of her.'

'Bless her. You're so lucky with her. She's such a poppet!'

'I know.' Ashley checks the time on her phone. 'She's been down for about an hour already and although she mostly sleeps through, a little drink of milk will soothe her and send her back off if she does happen to wake up. Which she won't! But you can call me if that happens. I'll keep checking my phone.'

'Listen, you. Just go out and enjoy yourself. Don't worry about me and Eden back here. We'll be fine. Tonight's about you. I haven't seen you like this, all ready for a night out, in ages. Just go!'

'I'll be back by one at the latest. I promise. Probably won't last that long, actually. It's been so long since I last went clubbing!'

'Don't worry about the time. It'll only just be getting going by then. I'll curl up here on the sofa, catch up on the soaps and then fall asleep. You get yourself on to that dance floor, girl.'

Ashley gives her friend an impetuous kiss on the forehead. 'Thanks, Kel. I owe you.'

It's nearly two o'clock in the morning by the time Ashley tumbles back through the doorway and rouses Kerry from her slumber on the couch.

'Kerry, Kerry. Wake up. You're not going to believe what's happened. I've had the best night ever.'

'What?'

'Don't be cross, Kel. I'm so sorry I'm late but I couldn't help it. I got chatting with someone. Someone nice. One of the partners involved in setting up the club. Like, one of the actual owners. I really like him!'

Kerry, drowsily shakes herself awake.

'That's brilliant, Ash. I'm really pleased you've met someone. Did you ask the cab to wait?'

'Yes, he's downstairs, holding on for you. And it's all paid for. Baz – that's his name – insisted that he took care of it. I'd suggest going down in the lift this time, though. Oh, Kerry, he's gorgeous. I think he could be the one. It's written in the stars!'

It is only once Kerry has gone and she has waved the taxi away (pointlessly from seven floors up because who could see the wave – but she *has* had a bit to drink and the thought makes her giggle) that she realises that she forgot to ask anything about Eden. Ashley dashes to the bedroom with a sudden pang of anxiety, but of course, Eden is sleeping peacefully.

In the morning, Ashley has a hangover. It presents itself firstly as a blinding pain over her right eye, along with a sticky mouth so parched of saliva it makes the Sahara seem more like the Amazon rainforest. Ashley lifts her head off the pillow but falls back down into the linen with a groan almost immediately. She is also starving hungry, she realises – but at the same time feels that there is absolutely no way she could put food into herself. She remembers now the way that cocaine does that to you.

But it is so, so worth it, no question. She has a little fizz in her stomach when she thinks about Baz. She clenches her sheet as a little rush of excitement shoots through her. They just seemed to hit it off completely. A line of cocaine in his private office meant that she was far more garrulous than usual. And gave her an inflated feeling of confidence. She felt like she could take on the world last night. Did she go back for a second? Possibly. In between the champagne and cocktails it is a bit of a blur. But Baz, Baz, Baz – he's gorgeous. The name buzzes round her mouth.

She looks over to the corner of the small room. Eden is smiling up at her from between the bars of her cot, full of joy and a baby's natural exuberance in readiness for a new day.

'Yes, my darling, you are very gorgeous too!'

Eden bounces up and down hard on the mattress in reply.

'Can I have some of your energy, love?' Ashley asks and grins back at her daughter, but it turns into a wince as the pincer-pain grips her forehead. It's the first hangover she's had in a couple of years – since before she was pregnant. She groans.

'Oh, God. I'd forgotten what this was like. I'm not sure that I have the energy to be Mum today…'

She rolls over in bed, turning away from her daughter for a moment. Though Eden can't possibly understand, something in Ashley doesn't want Eden to see her like this – the dregs of last night's makeup smeared across her face and staining the pillow, and her brain not quite functioning at full capacity.

Pull yourself together, she thinks. And then she notices the delicate flower, nestling on her pillow: a white orchid, given to her by Baz. 'It represents beauty and elegance,' he had whispered to her. 'Perfect for you.' She experiences a little tremor, an echo of the shiver that went through her last night as he said it.

And then she experiences another little jolt, remembering something that she read yesterday. She scrolls to check Christina's update. Yes, there it is: *A flower will become significant.*

Oh yes, indeed. It gives her just the little lift she needs. Ashley soon finds herself dragging a reluctant body from the bed and fixing breakfast for Eden. She wills herself not to look at her phone repeatedly, but the temptation is too much for her. And there it is, already. A message from Baz. Her stomach does a little flip that has nothing to do with the hangover.

Morning gorgeous. Really enjoyed last night. Can't wait to see you again. B

Yes. It all really happened and wasn't a figment of her imagination, and he likes her! She feels the thrill of being a teenager again, embarking on an adventure. So different from the recent drudgery of motherhood.

True, she didn't mention that she was a single mother with a one-year-old child stuck in a seventh floor flat, but there was plenty of time to see how this panned out before getting into the finer details of her domestic arrangements. Last night it had felt brilliant to just be like all the other girls in that club – young and carefree – if only for a few hours. A bit like Cinderella, she thinks, noticing Eden's fairytale book lying open on the floor. But with no intention of letting my carriage turn into a pumpkin.

Christina's daily text pings in:

There's something different about you today. Everyone will notice your newfound radiance. You've set the wheels in motion for enormous change. Now sit back and let it happen.

Oh, she's so right again. There's a lot in this psychic business. But wait, does that mean she shouldn't text Baz back? Before she can make up her mind a second message flashes up from him.

So, can I tempt you back tonight for more of the same? Think we should get to know each other a little better.

It's already happening, thinks Ashley. My life *is* changing. My luck is changing. She wants nothing more than to dance the night away with Baz again. Would Kerry babysit for a second night in a row? It's a pretty big ask – Friday *and* Saturday night. But why not? How long has it been since Ashley has had a big weekend? Kerry can have one whenever she likes. She isn't tied down by the responsibility of bringing up a child by herself. She's a good friend. She'll understand how important this is.

Kerry's reply isn't as enthusiastic as the previous day, but she agrees.

Alright babe, as it's you. Don't go making a habit of this, though!

Ashley's hangover seems to be lifting. She decides on a slightly teasing reply.

Might swing by later – if u r lucky. A x

It's ever so much more nonchalant in tone than she feels inside, but she's determined to play it cool this time – sit back and let it happen.

It is another brilliant night. Another later return than she promised to Kerry. Another free taxi ride home. Another few lines of cocaine. Another hangover. But again, it is worth it. And Baz is such a gentleman. He won't let her buy a drink. And, although he angled to be invited back to Ashley's, he didn't push it when she said she wasn't ready. She has had two of the best nights she has ever experienced and they haven't cost her a penny. Ashley feels as if life is suddenly starting to *happen* to her. Just as Christina – and the newspaper horoscope – predicted it would.

The pattern repeats itself the following weekend, but Kerry is already fed up with being asked to babysit. She will do the Friday night, but not the Saturday. Both weekend nights for two weekends in a row is a bit much. Ashley knows that she is pushing it by even asking, but she is desperate to see Baz, and surprised by how much she is loving getting back to the clubbing scene. She simply has to go out Saturday night as well. She *has* to. She still hasn't told Baz about Eden. The pumping music of the club isn't exactly conducive to cosy chats on awkward subjects.

She tries another friend to babysit for her. It's awkward to ask Hollie out of the blue. She hasn't spoken to her for months. To her relief, Hollie agrees. She has only met Eden a couple of times – but Eden is a friendly, accommodating little thing and it all goes well.

By the fifth weekend, Ashley has well and truly exhausted all of her babysitting options. But not seeing Baz is not an option either. She has never felt like this about anyone before. Ever. Every day begins with a kind of fluttery excitement and anticipation. But it is more than that. Baz is central to it, but it is the whole scene at the club. The dancing and the drugs – which are completely under control, just a line here and a dab there to give her a little buzz – have brought back the meaning of fun. And they mean that she is in great shape. For the first time in a few years Ashley knows that she looks good. Really good. And looking good has kickstarted the confidence that had been so lacking lately. If she's honest, since Eden was born.

Ashley has even stopped taking notice of Christina's daily messages and psychic updates, and no longer jumps to the horoscope pages online or in the magazines. A flower has indeed been very significant: Ashley glances at the orchid on the window ledge, but there is no need to rely on all of that anymore.

The whole thing has made her a better mum, too, Ashley is certain. There are fewer hangovers now that she is getting back into the pace of the clubbing scene, and an inner confidence along with that outer glow. It has given her the spur she needed to try a few things. She has baked fairy cakes with Eden standing by, allowing her to plunge her pudgy fingers into the mix and 'help'. They have under-taken some arty projects together; Ashley is rediscovering her creative side. And they leave the flat every single day now, Ashley makes sure of that. To the shops, to the park, even to the woods sometimes. The fresh air is doing them both good, and there is always a spring in Ashley's step as she pushes the stroller around.

Everyone has commented on Ashley's transformation. Her social circle has widened dramatically because of the club – and her elevated status that comes through being connected to Baz. Her Baz is the golden boy. There is a sense of pride, for Ashley, in his achievements. He has turned that place around in such a short space of time. The White Orchid is a success. Numbers on the door are up week on week. Ashley scrolls through the pictures from last weekend, noting with some satisfaction the perfection of her own new acrylic nails, paid for by Baz – a gift for helping him through these difficult first few weeks of opening.

She is young. She is single. But not free. There is Eden. Which brings Ashley right back to the babysitting problem.

Her phone pings with a message from Kerry. *Time for that catch up yet?*

Not if you can't babysit, Ashley thinks.

She has already half made the decision.

Ashley is out of other options.

Eden sleeps so well that she never wakes up and *always sleeps through*. Ashley can't actually remember the last time she had to go to her in the night. If she is only going to be out for a couple of hours – the club doesn't really get going until about 11pm, and she can be back home by around three in the morning, what if she simply leaves Eden home alone? The plan develops through the day, but Ashley realises that she has been considering it for a few weeks now. Eden could be tucked into the wardrobe in the bedroom so that no harm can come to her (and the neighbours can't hear if she does wake up, which she won't).

Ashley does the bedtime story inside the wardrobe with Eden – makes a game of it, in fact. She fixes the little Upsy Daisy nightlight on a timer on a shelf inside the wardrobe so that Eden isn't going to sleep in the dark, places the mattress on the floor where it fits perfectly, and arranges all Eden's teddies around the edges so that it is soft and cosy. She also makes sure that she doesn't even start to get ready until Eden is long asleep – so that her daughter has no idea.

It is another fantastic night at the club, though Ashley is on edge the whole time. When the taxi drops her off in the early hours of the morning there is a slightly sickly feeling in the pit of Ashley's stomach. She has nothing to worry about: inside the wardrobe, Eden is sleeping soundly, oblivious to all.

Also by Mirror Books

Stella's Story
Louise Allen

"Stella is just like a tiny bird. This is my first impression of her. A quiet little sparrow of a girl."

In the first of a new series 'Thrown Away Children', foster mother Louise Allen tells the true story of Stella, a young girl scarred by an abusive past.

Named for the lager that christened her, Stella's life is characterised by dysfunction and neglect. Her mother abandons her as a newborn and in the 'care' of her father, Stella is left with no food, water, clothes or warmth.

Louise becomes Stella's foster carer and is determined to give the girl a better life. But when Stella has a startling response to having her photo taken, it is clear that the effects of her abuse run deep.

m
B
MIRROR BOOKS